1500 General Knowledge Quiz Questions and Answers

by

Terry Dolan

Quiz 1

1. According to Greek mythology, who was the first woman on earth?
2. The Green Goblin is the archenemy of which superhero?
3. Addis Ababa is the capital of which country?
4. At what number degrees Fahrenheit does water freeze?
5. For which country is the beaver a national emblem?
6. What is the name of TS Eliot's railway cat?
7. STR is the airport code of which city?
8. How is the gas Nitrous Oxide better known?
9. Baltimore is the largest city in which US state?
10. How many English kings have been called William?
11. What is the pen name of the author Barbara Vine?
12. In cartoons, at what store did Wile E. Coyote buy his merchandise?
13. How many letters are there in the German alphabet?
14. In Scrabble how many points is the letter C worth?
15. The Boxer Rebellion took place in which country?

Quiz 1 Answers

1. Pandora
2. Spiderman
3. Ethiopia
4. 32
5. Canada
6. Shimbleshanks
7. Stuttgart
8. Laughing gas
9. Maryland
10. 4
11. Ruth Rendell
12. Acme
13. 30
14. 3
15. China

Quiz 2

1. In geometry what instrument is used to measure angles?
2. From which country do vehicles bearing the international index mark GBZ come from?
3. A gnu is another name for which animal?
4. According to legend which one of Henry VIII's wives had six fingers on one hand?
5. Hairy nosed and Queensland are both varieties of which animal?
6. Who was the author of Swallows and Amazons?
7. How many players are there in a baseball team?
8. In the television series The Dukes of Hazzard which actress played the role of Daisy Duke?
9. How many time zones are there in the contiguous USA?
10. In The Jungle Book, who was leader of the wolves?
11. How many Popes have taken the name Innocent?
12. Who is the patron saint of Germany?
13. In 1960, which country became the first in the world to have a female Prime Minister?
14. Kampuchea is the former name of which modern-day name country?
15. In what do arboreal creatures live?

Quiz 2 Answers

1. Protractor
2. Gibraltar
3. Wildebeest
4. Anne Boleyn
5. Wombat
6. Arthur Ransome
7. 9
8. Catherine Bach
9. 4
10. Akala
11. 13

12. Boniface
13. Sri Lanka
14. Cambodia
15. Trees

Quiz 3

1. Karl Marx spent the last 34 years of his life in which country?
2. Orly airport is situated in which European city?
3. What is the name of Batman's butler?
4. How many players are there in a rugby league team?
5. The song Ding Dong the Witch Is Dead featured in which movie?
6. Lisbon stands on which river?
7. Of what is acoustiphobia the fear?
8. How many sides does a rhombus have?
9. Scotch, Rye and Bourbon are all types of which drink?
10. The instrument that measures wind speed has what name?
11. Who wrote the novel The Silence of the Lambs?
12. How many different categories are there in each version of Trivial Pursuit?
13. God speed your love to me is the final line in which song?
14. Marcel Marceau is associated with which art form?
15. Masked, Hermit and Spider are all types of which animal?

Quiz 3 Answers

1. England
2. Paris
3. Alfred
4. 13
5. The Wizard of Oz
6. Tagus
7. Noise

8. 4
9. Whisky
10. Anemometer
11. Thomas Harris
12. 6
13. Unchained Melody
14. Mime
15. Crab

Quiz 4

1. Montevideo stands on which river?
2. Of what is alektorophobia the fear?
3. Monkswell Manor is the setting for which long running stage play?
4. A duiker is what type of animal?
5. How many operas did Ludwig van Beethoven write?
6. Which British football club are nicknamed The Railwaymen?
7. Coulrophobia is the fear of what?
8. Which US city is known as the City of Brotherly Love?
9. How many Graces are there in Greek mythology?
10. Which city is the administrative headquarters of Cornwall?
11. In mythology who was the father of Romulus and Remus?
12. On which island is Mount Etna?
13. How many holes are there on a golf course?
14. In an Italian restaurant, what are grissini?
15. Which cartoon character is described as "the fastest mouse in all Mexico"?

Quiz 4 Answers

1. Plate
2. Chickens
3. The Mousetrap

4. Antelope
5. 1
6. Crewe Alexandra
7. Clowns
8. Philadelphia
9. 3
10. Truro
11. Mars
12. Sicily
13. 18
14. Breadsticks
15. Speedy Gonzales

Quiz 5

1. Who created the literary sleuth Brother Cadfael?
2. Which London bridge connects St Paul's Cathedral and the Tate Modern?
3. Humphrey Bogart played the character Charlie Allnut in which movie?
4. In which TV series did Sarah Jessica Parker play the role of Carrie Bradshaw?
5. A descent is the collective noun for which bird?
6. Of what is iatrophobia the fear?
7. Who wrote The Murders in the Rue Morgue?
8. Estoril is the venue of which Formula One Grand Prix?
9. Ethiopia had what former name?
10. From which fruit is perry made?
11. If you were sticking or twisting what game would you be playing?
12. In 1881 Carol I became the first king of which country?
13. During World War One who was the President of the USA?
14. For what does E stand for in ETA?
15. Who was the lead vocalist of the glam rock group Wizzard?

Quiz 5 Answers

1. Ellis Peters
2. Millennium Bridge
3. The African Queen
4. Sex and the City
5. Woodpecker
6. Doctors
7. Edgar Allan Poe
8. Portuguese
9. Abyssinia
10. Pears
11. Pontoon
12. Romania
13. Woodrow Wilson
14. Estimated
15. Roy Wood

Quiz 6

1. A basilisk is what type of creature?
2. The dish paella originates from which country?
3. What colour follows an orange belt in judo?
4. Who is the arch enemy of Flash Gordon?
5. From which plant is linseed oil obtained?
6. Fuad 1 became king of which country in 1922?
7. Gamophobia is the fear of what?
8. How was jazz musician Thomas Waller better known?
9. In Gulliver's Travels what is the name of the land of the giants?
10. How was the heir to the French throne known?
11. The world's longest pier is in which English resort?
12. What is the surname of the Russian author after whom a park in Moscow is named?
13. In Scrabble how many points is the letter V worth?
14. Kigali is the capital city of which country?
15. Of what is somniphobia the fear?

Quiz 6 Answers

1. Lizard
2. Spain
3. Green
4. Ming The Merciless
5. Flax
6. Egypt
7. Marriage
8. Fats
9. Brobdingnag
10. Dauphin
11. Southend
12. Gorky
13. 4
14. Rwanda
15. Sleep

Quiz 7

1. Which electrician won the Nobel Peace Prize in 1983?
2. In cartoons who led the gang whose members included Benny the Ball and Choo Choo?
3. Which saint's day is celebrated on Boxing Day?
4. Which British city is home to the Heriot-Watt University?
5. What is the capital of Kosovo?
6. South-West Africa is now known by which name?
7. Which US city is nicknamed Little Cuba?
8. The city of Bratislava is in which European country?
9. In which movie did Whoopi Goldberg dress as a nun?
10. Hg is the chemical symbol for which element?
11. How is pugilism better known?
12. What is the only French city that stands on the River Rhine?
13. Who wrote the novel King Solomon's Mines?
14. How many lines are there in a sonnet?

15. In which city was Archduke Franz Ferdinand assassinated in 1914, the event that sparked WW1?

Quiz 7 Answers

1. Lech Walesa
2. Top Cat
3. St Stephen
4. Edinburgh
5. Pristina
6. Namibia
7. Miami
8. Slovakia
9. Sister Act
10. Mercury
11. Boxing
12. Strasbourg
13. H Rider Haggard
14. 14
15. Sarajevo

Quiz 8

1. Belgrade was the capital of which former country?
2. Bellis perennis is more commonly known as which wild flower?
3. Benito Mussolini was the leader of which country?
4. Bernadotte is the family name of which country's royal house?
5. The King and I was set in which country?
6. Who was the first woman to be appointed head of MI5?
7. In Ancient Greece who acquired the nickname of The Father of Medicine?
8. How many pints of blood are there in the average adult human body?
9. Lloyd George, Norfolk Giant and Newbury are all varieties of which fruit?

10. Located in Russia near the border with Georgia, what is the highest mountain in Europe?
11. Pathophobia the fear of what?
12. Amman is the capital of which country?
13. In Greek mythology which of the Muses was the goddess of love poetry?
14. How many tentacles does a squid have?
15. How was Bangladesh formerly known?

Quiz 8 Answers

1. Yugoslavia
2. Daisy
3. Italy
4. Sweden
5. Siam
6. Stella Rimington
7. Hippocrates
8. 9
9. Raspberry
10. Elbrus
11. Illness
12. Jordan
13. Erato
14. 10
15. East Pakistan

Quiz 9

1. Huey, Dewey and Louie are the nephews of which cartoon character?
2. Hydrogen burns in air to form what?
3. A bee normally has how many wings?
4. According to the song how many trombones were there in the big parade?
5. What species of ape are native to the Rock of Gibraltar?
6. In Greek Mythology how many heads did the Hydra have?

7. Who wrote the novel The War of the Worlds?
8. In 1966 who was elected Governor of California?
9. How many notes are there in the musical scale?
10. Paris stands on which river?
11. Peace, Just Joey and Whisky Mac are all varieties of what?
12. Of whom is Dominic the patron saint?
13. Who invented a code made up of dots and dashes?
14. What is the principal colour of the Moroccan flag?
15. Cairo stands near the mouth of which river?

Quiz 9 Answers

1. Donald Duck
2. Water
3. 4
4. 76
5. Barbary
6. 9
7. HG Wells
8. Ronald Reagan
9. 7
10. Seine
11. Rose
12. Astronomers
13. Samuel Morse
14. Red
15. Nile

Quiz 10

1. Which musical note goes before soh?
2. Romeo and Juliet was a top 10 hit in 1981 for which band?
3. In tennis which stadium hosts the French Open?
4. In the Noddy stories what is the name of the policeman?

5. Found in the rainforests of Southeast Asia what is the name of the world's largest flower?
6. From what is ghee made?
7. How many types of chess pieces are there in a standard set?
8. Curry gets its colouring from which herb?
9. What is the name of the parliament of the Isle of Man?
10. Who wrote the novel Uncle Tom's Cabin?
11. How many colours are there in the rainbow?
12. Crested, smooth and palmate are all types of what?
13. Dakar is the capital of which African country?
14. Dodge City is located in which US State?
15. How many verses are there in the Greek national anthem?

Quiz 10 Answers

1. Fah
2. Dire Straits
3. Roland Garros
4. PC Plod
5. Rafflesia
6. Butter
7. 6
8. Turmeric
9. Tynwald
10. Harriet Beecher Stowe
11. 7
12. Newt
13. Senegal
14. Kansas
15. 138

Quiz 11

1.   In Ancient Greece where was the most important oracle located?
2.   Cirrus or cumulus are examples of?
3.   In George Orwell's Animal Farm what type of animal was Napoleon?
4.   Cl is the symbol of which chemical element?
5.   Columcille is the middle name of which actor?
6.   In Greek mythology the winged horse Pegasus sprang from the body of whom after her death?
7.   How many sunflowers are there in Vincent Van Gogh's famous painting?
8.   If a dish is cooked Florentine, what is it cooked with?
9.   In 1885, William Le Baron Jenney built the world's first skyscraper in which city?
10. Lutetia was the Roman name of which European city?
11. The character Newman Noggs features in which Charles Dickens novel?
12. What animal is the symbol of the motor manufacturer Suzuki?
13. Who composed The Wedding March?
14. What is the alternative title of Schubert's 8th Symphony?
15. Daytona Beach is in which US state?

Quiz 11 Answers

1.   Delphi
2.   Cloud
3.   Pig
4.   Chlorine
5.   Mel Gibson
6.   Medusa
7.   15
8.   Spinach
9.   Chicago
10. Paris

11. Nicholas Nickleby
12. Rhinoceros
13. Felix Mendelssohn
14. The Unfinished Symphony
15. Florida

Quiz 12

1. A cow that has not had a calf is called what?
2. Hierro, Gomera and Fuerteventura are part of which island group?
3. According to Greek mythology who was the wife of Odysseus?
4. Homer's epic poems, The Iliad and The Odyssey, are made up of how many books each?
5. Acrophobia is the fear of what?
6. Lusitania was the Roman name for which European country?
7. How is German Measles also known?
8. The Black Forest is in which European country?
9. Lord Voldemort killed the parents of which famous literary character?
10. The television series M*A*S*H was set during which war?
11. Miracle, kelvedon wonder and meteor are all types of which vegetable?
12. An elver will grow into what creature?
13. Anser Anser is the scientific name for which bird?
14. Insulin is produced in which organ of the body?
15. Nutria is the fur of which animal?

Quiz 12 Answers

1. Heifer
2. Canary
3. Penelope
4. 24

5. Horses
6. Portugal
7. Rubella
8. Germany
9. Harry Potter
10. Korean
11. Pea
12. Eel
13. Greylag Goose
14. Pancreas
15. Coypu

Quiz 13

1. In Greek mythology who was the goddess of the moon?
2. What is the Cockney rhyming slang for flowers?
3. In the Harry Potter movies which character is played by Alan Rickman?
4. What is the national bird of India?
5. Yen is the national currency of which country?
6. In computing, which word is used for binary digit?
7. How many countries does the Sahara desert cover?
8. Which short British engineer used to wear a huge top hat in a bid to make himself look taller?
9. Who founded the Boy Scouts?
10. In boxing who was the first to defeat Mike Tyson in a professional bout?
11. Which nursery rhyme character "could eat no fat"?
12. As whom is the fictional character Princess Aurora better known?
13. Captain Hastings is the assistant of which fictional detective?
14. Who discovered Uranus in 1781?
15. A pintail is what type of bird?

Quiz 13 Answers

1. Artemis
2. April showers
3. Severus Snape
4. Peacock
5. Japan
6. Bit
7. 11
8. Isambard Kingdom Brunel
9. Robert Baden Powell
10. James "Buster" Douglas
11. Jack Sprat
12. Sleeping Beauty
13. Hercule Poirot
14. William Herschel
15. Duck

Quiz 14

1. Actor John Wayne had what nickname?
2. According to the superstition how many lives does a cat have?
3. By what name is sportsman Edson Arantes do Nascimento better known?
4. Saintpaulia is the Latin name for which popular houseplant?
5. Which Nursery Rhyme character sat on a tuffet?
6. How is the airborne Australian medical service more commonly known?
7. In which yacht did Sir Francis Chichester sail solo around the world?
8. Goatsucker is the North American name for which bird?
9. P.C. Wren was the author of which novel about the French Foreign Legion?
10. Italian Reinhold Messner made the 1st successful solo ascent of Mount Everest in which year?

11. How many periods of play are there in a game of ice hockey?
12. In literature the character of Oliver Mellors is better known as whom?
13. Globe and Jerusalem are types of what?
14. Gold Coast was the former name of what African nation?
15. The word karaoke comes from which language?

Quiz 14 Answers

1. Duke
2. 9
3. Pele
4. African violet
5. Little Miss Muffet
6. Flying Doctor
7. Gipsy Moth
8. Nightjar
9. Beau Geste
10. 1980
11. 3
12. Lady Chatterley's Lover
13. Artichoke
14. Ghana
15. Japanese

Quiz 15

1. Which cartoon TV series features a pair of brothers called Rock and Gravel?
2. Ray Kroc established which fast food restaurant?
3. In what language does obrigado mean thank you?
4. In which year did the liner the Titanic sink?
5. For what does the Y stand in DIY?
6. Gurkha soldiers come from which country?
7. Author of 'Dracula,' what was Bram Stoker's first name an abbreviation of?

8. The Aztecs of Mexico spoke which language?
9. The Black Sea is off the north coast of which country?
10. There are how many players in a cricket team?
11. What is the capital of Ecuador?
12. When did the first man go into space?
13. Catherine the Great was born in which country?
14. By what name is singer Gordon Sumner better known?
15. Catoptrophobia is the fear of what?

Quiz 15 Answers

1. Wacky Races
2. McDonalds
3. Portuguese
4. 1912
5. Yourself
6. Nepal
7. Abraham
8. Nahuatl
9. Turkey
10. 11
11. Quito
12. 1961
13. Poland
14. Sting
15. Mirrors

Quiz 16

1. Charles Lutwidge Dodgson was the real name of which author?
2. Who was the wife of King Louis XVI of France?
3. Dutch Guiana is the former name of which country?
4. Edmonton is the capital of which Canadian province?
5. Who writes fantasy novels about Discworld?
6. Behind the Nile and the Amazon, what is the third longest river in the world?

7. For his role in which movie did Jeff Bridges win the 2010 Academy Award for Best Actor?
8. Duffle coats are named after a town in which country?
9. All children except one grow up is the first line of which story?
10. Also the name of an English city, Harare, the capital of Zimbabwe was known as what until 1987?
11. Cranesbill is the wild form of which garden flower?
12. Bird's Nest Soup is associated with which country?
13. Dystychiphobia is the fear of what?
14. How is a modulator-demodulator better known?
15. Beta-blockers stop secretion of what chemical?

Quiz 16 Answers

1. Lewis Carroll
2. Marie Antoinette
3. Suriname
4. Alberta
5. Terry Pratchett
6. Mississippi
7. Crazy Heart
8. Belgium
9. Peter Pan
10. Salisbury
11. Geranium
12. China
13. Accidents
14. Modem
15. Adrenaline

Quiz 17

1. Bob Hawke was Prime Minister of which country?
2. The Olympic flame always starts its journey in which city?
3. From which fish does caviar come?
4. How many countries make up Scandinavia?

5. Hydrophobia the fear of what?
6. In athletics what name is given to the event with ten different track and field challenges?
7. In Greek Mythology, how many heads did the dog Cerberus who guarded the entrance to Hades have?
8. Canton is the former name of which Chinese city?
9. In the phonetic alphabet, what word represents the letter S?
10. Which actor played the role of President Jed Bartlet in the TV drama The West Wing?
11. Of which bird is the collective noun a murmuration?
12. Baghdad is the capital of which country?
13. Giovanni Agnelli founded which Italian car company?
14. Granite stones are used in which winter sport?
15. Which town in West Bengal gave its name to a high quality tea?

Quiz 17 Answers

1. Australia
2. Athens
3. Sturgeon
4. 4
5. Water
6. Decathlon
7. 3
8. Guangzhou
9. Sierra
10. Martin Sheen
11. Starling
12. Iraq
13. Fiat
14. Curling
15. Darjeeling

Quiz 18

1. Bright's disease affects which organs of the body?
2. Who sailed to the Galapagos Islands on his ship HMS Beagle?
3. Bucharest is the capital of which country?
4. What is the common name for the clavicle?
5. Buck and Doe are the male and female terms for which animal?
6. How many boroughs are there in the city of New York?
7. After which US president was the teddy bear named?
8. Which famous historical person was assassinated by John Wilkes Booth?
9. Bulgaria has what basic unit of currency?
10. Which female pop singer had a big hit called Baby, One More Time?
11. By what name is Reginald Dwight better known?
12. Common, Water and Pygmy are types of which British mammal?
13. What do the French call the English Channel?
14. Which physicist wrote a book called A Brief History of Time?
15. Edward Ferrars and Elinor Dashwood are characters in which novel?

Quiz 18 Answers

1. Kidneys
2. Charles Darwin
3. Romania
4. The collar bone
5. Rabbit
6. 5
7. Theodore Roosevelt
8. Abraham Lincoln
9. Lev
10. Britney Spears
11. Elton John

12. Shrew
13. La Manche
14. Stephen Hawking
15. Sense and Sensibility

Quiz 19

1. A match of three games of bridge is called what?
2. A Methuselah of wine holds the equivalent of how many bottles?
3. Which cartoon bird was the object of cat Sylvester's plans?
4. Fe is the symbol for which chemical element?
5. In what year were the Tiananmen Square protests in which an estimated 3,000 pro-democracy students were killed?
6. From whom did Shylock take his pound of flesh?
7. Gaborone is the capital of which country?
8. Genealogy is the study of a family's what?
9. General Franco became dictator of which country in 1939?
10. The Greek island Corfu is geographically closest to which country?
11. Cottage, Vienna and French stick are all types of what?
12. Crabs, lobsters and shrimps are all members of which class of creature?
13. For how many minutes did Andy Warhol say everyone would be famous?
14. As whom was Lev Davidovitch Bronstein better known?
15. Asia Minor was a great peninsula of west Asia making up most of which modern country?

Quiz 19 Answers

1. Rubber
2. 8
3. Tweetie Pie

4. Iron
5. 1989
6. Antonio
7. Botswana
8. History
9. Spain
10. Albania
11. Bread
12. Crustacean
13. 15
14. Trotsky
15. Turkey

Quiz 20

1. A pollack is a member of which family of fish?
2. A skulk is the collective noun for which animal?
3. Leonberger, Affenpinscher and Keeshond and are all types of what?
4. Of what is spheksophobia the fear?
5. Ailurophobia is the fear of what?
6. After which god is Wednesday named?
7. The Serpentine lake is in which London park?
8. Who wrote the novel The Water Babies?
9. Of what was Juventas the Roman goddess?
10. What is the name given to the study of reptiles?
11. How many wives did English King Henry VIII divorce?
12. Captain Robert Falcon Scott and his expedition reached the South Pole in January of which year?
13. How many locks are there in the Panama Canal?
14. After 27 years in prison Nelson Mandela was freed in which year?
15. In Greek mythology, who was the daughter of Zeus and Leda?

Quiz 20 Answers

1. Cod
2. Fox
3. Dog
4. Wasps
5. Cats
6. Woden
7. Hyde Park
8. Charles Kingsley
9. Youth
10. Herpetology
11. 2
12. 1912
13. 6
14. 1990
15. Helen

Quiz 21

1. Of which bird can the collective noun be either a building or a clamour?
2. Caracas is the capital of which country?
3. What is the alternative title of Piano Sonata No 14 by Beethoven?
4. In geography what is Rapa Nui better known as?
5. How many wheels does a Hansom cab have?
6. In mythology Pan was half man and half which animal?
7. Biro who invented the first mass-produced ballpoint pen had what first name?
8. What is the groove under the nose called?
9. Helvetia is another name for which country?
10. How high in feet is a basketball hoop from the floor?
11. What type of creature is a tanager?
12. Which capital city is the same as its principality's name?
13. Which other name is used for the puma or mountain lion?

14. The city of Berlin stands on which river?
15. In the old American West, what was Boot Hill?

Quiz 21 Answers

1. Rook
2. Venezuela
3. Moonlight
4. Easter Island
5. 2
6. Goat
7. Lazlo
8. Philtrum
9. Switzerland
10. 10
11. Bird
12. Luxembourg
13. Cougar
14. Spree
15. Cemetery

Quiz 22

1. Which is the only bird that can fly backwards?
2. What name is given to a mixture of wet straw and leaves, spread to protect the leaves of newly planted trees?
3. A racehorse that has never won a race is given what name?
4. What is the currency unit of Libya?
5. In what year did the "Gunfight at the OK Corral" take place?
6. Which singer, nicknamed The Little Sparrow, died in 1963 aged 48?
7. The Night Watch was painted by which Dutch artist?
8. Which country's football teams play in the Bundesliga?
9. Who was the director of the movie Psycho?

10. The fictional character Miss Marple was created by which author?
11. "The first place that I can well remember was a large pleasant meadow with a pond of clear water in it" is the first line of which novel?
12. What was the name of the Lone Ranger's horse?
13. The shinbone has what medical name?
14. Phil and Don were members of which 50's singing duo?
15. Which element is used in vulcanising rubber?

Quiz 22 Answers

1. Hummingbird
2. Mulch
3. Maiden
4. Dinar
5. 1881
6. Edith Piaf
7. Rembrandt
8. Germany
9. Alfred Hitchcock
10. Agatha Christie
11. Black Beauty
12. Silver
13. Tibia
14. Everly
15. Sulphur

Quiz 23

1. Ag is the chemical symbol for which metal?
2. Amathophobia is the fear of what?
3. Cairo is the capital city of which country?
4. By what name is the spiny anteater otherwise known?
5. What is the capital of US state Rhode Island?
6. A dinner jacket in Britain what is this garment called in America?

7. What is the third letter of the Greek alphabet?
8. A float is the collective noun for a group of what?
9. What is the last book of the Bible?
10. Who was circus boss Barnum's partner?
11. In which English county is the Lake District?
12. Merton College is part of which UK University?
13. Who is the patron saint of Paris, France?
14. A convict called Magwitch appeared in which Charles Dickens's novel?
15. Which gas makes up the biggest fraction of air?

Quiz 23 Answers

1. Silver
2. Dust
3. Egypt
4. Echidna
5. Providence
6. Tuxedo
7. Gamma
8. Crocodiles
9. Revelation
10. Bailey
11. Cumbria
12. Oxford
13. Genevieve
14. Great Expectations
15. Nitrogen

Quiz 24

1. A Granny Smith is a variety of what fruit?
2. A slice of which fruit is traditionally served with fish?
3. April 25th is which national holiday in Australia and New Zealand?
4. Arithmophobia is the fear of what?
5. As is the chemical symbol for which element?
6. Batman is based in which city?

7. Bogota is the capital city of which country?
8. Which actress began life as Doris Kapellhoff?
9. Which acid is found in an ant's sting?
10. In which year was President Kennedy assassinated?
11. What is the literal meaning of `pince-nez' glasses?
12. German dramatist Brecht had what first name?
13. Which fish has a variety called skipjack?
14. Lundi is the French name for which day?
15. Where were the 1936 Olympics held?

Quiz 24 Answers

1. Apple
2. Lemon
3. Anzac Day
4. Numbers
5. Arsenic
6. Gotham
7. Colombia
8. Doris Day
9. Formic
10. 1963
11. Pinch-nose
12. Bertolt
13. Tuna
14. Monday
15. Berlin

Quiz 25

1. A sol is a silver coin of what country?
2. What popular dog name means 'faithful' in Latin?
3. At which battle of 1515 was King James IV of Scotland killed?
4. Actor and comedian Bob Hope had what real first name?
5. What number do the Roman numerals CC represent?

6. Which musical features the song, "Ah Yes I Remember It Well"?
7. According to Shakespeare what type of snake killed Cleopatra?
8. Augusta is the state capital of which US state?
9. By what name is the patella commonly called?
10. What did Karl Marx describe as the opiate of the people?
11. In the Dirty Harry series of movies what is the surname of the character played by Clint Eastwood?
12. What nationality was scientist Marie Curie?
13. Vivien Leigh and Joan Plowright were the wives of which actor?
14. On which continent is Sierra Leone?
15. How many counties make up Northern Ireland?

Quiz 25 Answers

1. Peru
2. Fido
3. Flodden
4. Leslie
5. 200
6. Gigi
7. Asp
8. Maine
9. Kneecap
10. Religion
11. Callahan
12. Polish
13. Laurence Olivier
14. Africa
15. 6

Quiz 26

1. The character Scout Finch appeared in which novel?
2. Archibald Leach was the real name of which actor?
3. What would a toxicologist study?
4. Crampons are used in which sport?
5. When translated, what dinosaur name means "three-horned face"?
6. Asmara is the capital city of which country?
7. The Aswan High Dam is on which river?
8. Which US state is nicknamed the Bluegrass state?
9. Who wrote Auld Lang Syne?
10. A sousaphone is a large bass version of which musical instrument?
11. John Paul I, who held the Papacy for one month, died in which year?
12. The prefix gastro refers to which bodily organ?
13. Roman emperor Caligula made which animal a senator?
14. In which country is the world's highest waterfall?
15. "Call me Ishmael" is the first line of which novel?

Quiz 26 Answers

1. To Kill a Mockingbird
2. Cary Grant
3. Poisons
4. Climbing
5. Triceratops
6. Eritrea
7. Nile
8. Kentucky
9. Robert Burns
10. Tuba
11. 1978
12. Stomach
13. Horse
14. Venezuela
15. Moby Dick

Quiz 27

1. A taipan is what type of creature?
2. By what name was Grigory Efimovich better known in early 20th century Russia?
3. Bridgetown is the capital of which country?
4. Ceylon is the former name of which country?
5. Chionophobia is the fear of what?
6. For what does the S stand in NASA?
7. How many days a week did the Beatles sing about?
8. A chough is what type of creature?
9. Charles, the first pilot to exceed the speed of sound, had what surname?
10. What was the American codename for the development of the atom bomb?
11. What was the surname of US WW2 general George, who was known as 'Old Blood and Guts?'
12. Chomolungma is also known as which mountain?
13. With which sport is Billie-Jean King associated?
14. From which language did Afrikaans develop?
15. For how many minutes does a round in professional boxing last?

Quiz 27 Answers

1. Snake
2. Rasputin
3. Barbados
4. Sri Lanka
5. Snow
6. Space
7. 8
8. Bird
9. Yeager
10. Manhattan Project
11. Patton
12. Everest
13. Tennis

14. Dutch
15. 3

Quiz 28

1. For what type of music is Johann Strauss known?
2. By what name is Stanley Burrell better known in the music world?
3. Which female icon did Ruth Handler create in 1959?
4. Marengo was the horse of which famous soldier?
5. Which fibre is taken from the Angora goat?
6. How is dichlorodiphenyltrichloroethane better known?
7. A pregnant goldfish is given which name?
8. The character Catherine Earnshaw appeared in which novel?
9. From which island do Sards come?
10. What would a bibliophile collect?
11. Who developed the theory of relativity?
12. In which sport can you throw a curve ball?
13. Which South American country has the greatest land area?
14. What title did the rulers of ancient Egypt assume?
15. A corvid is what type of animal?

Quiz 28 Answers

1. Waltzes
2. MC Hammer
3. Barbie
4. Napoleon
5. Mohair
6. DDT
7. Twit
8. Wuthering Heights
9. Sardinia
10. Books
11. Albert Einstein
12. Baseball

13. Brazil
14. Pharaoh
15. Bird

Quiz 29

1. At what age does a filly become a mare?
2. Which Greek dish is made mainly from aubergines and lamb?
3. At the beginning of a game of backgammon how many counters does each player have?
4. How is the German Shepherd dog otherwise known?
5. According to Douglas Adams's novel The Hitch Hiker's Guide to the Galaxy, what number was the answer to "Life, the Universe and Everything"?
6. Which group had hits in the 1970s with Crazy Horses and Love Me for a Reason?
7. Boston is the capital of which US state?
8. Raymond Burr played which disabled television detective?
9. Which disease, characterised by spasmodic contraction of muscles is also called Lockjaw?
10. How is Peking now more commonly known?
11. How many ancient wonders of the world were there?
12. In the Rocky movies what was the surname of the title character?
13. What word can follow cart, race and hobby?
14. Who was the first woman to fly solo from England to Australia?
15. Morpheus was the Greek god of what?

Quiz 29 Answers

1. 4 years
2. Moussaka
3. 15
4. Alsatian
5. 42

6. Osmonds
7. Massachusetts
8. Ironside
9. Tetanus
10. Beijing
11. 7
12. Balboa
13. Horse
14. Amy Johnson
15. Dreams

Quiz 30

1. From what is the city of Petra carved?
2. Baseball player Babe Ruth's had what real first name?
3. Budapest is the capital city of which country?
4. For which country did Ian Smith claim independence?
5. By what name is the Alligator Pear better known?
6. Which character from A Midsummer Night's Dream shares his name with a piece of sporting equipment?
7. He is the symbol for which chemical element?
8. How many black squares are there on a chessboard?
9. What was the name of Tonto's horse?
10. What type of creature is a bushbuck?
11. New Zealand and Australia are separated by which sea?
12. Azoth is the alchemical name for which element?
13. What is the world's largest rodent?
14. Southfork ranch featured in which television series?
15. What is a young owl called?

Quiz 30 Answers

1. Rock
2. George
3. Hungary
4. Rhodesia
5. Avocado
6. Puck

7. Helium
8. 32
9. Scout
10. Antelope
11. Tasman
12. Mercury
13. Capybara
14. Dallas
15. Owlet

Quiz 31

1. By what nickname was William Bonney better known?
2. What is the capital city of Macedonia?
3. Of what is tachophobia the fear?
4. Actor Leonardo DiCaprio was born in November 11th of which year?
5. Who wrote the poem Paradise Lost?
6. What was the title of the 2003 animated movie that features a shark called Bruce?
7. Who is the Roman god of gates and doors?
8. Jeudi is the French word for which day?
9. What is the largest internal human organ?
10. Who invented the hot air balloon?
11. The discovery of Tutankhamen's tomb took place in the Valley of Kings near Luxor in Egypt in which year?
12. Who is Spiderman's alter ego?
13. All Blacks rugby team come from which country?
14. What number does the Roman numeral X stand for?
15. What sort of animal is a Borzoi?

Quiz 31 Answers

1. Billy The Kid
2. Skopje
3. Speed
4. 1974
5. John Milton

6. Finding Nemo
7. Janus
8. Thursday
9. Liver
10. Montgolfier brothers
11. 1922
12. Peter Parker
13. New Zealand
14. 10
15. Dog

Quiz 32

1. By what other name is the funny bone known?
2. Of what is chromatics the science?
3. In which year did the Live Aid pop concert, which was held in London and Philadelphia and raised money for famine relief in Africa, take place?
4. Which poet wrote The Pied Piper of Hamelin?
5. Who was the Greek goddess of the dawn?
6. In the comic strip The Perishers what is the name of the dog?
7. Of what is entomophobia the fear?
8. Islamabad is the capital of which country?
9. What is Fred Flintstone's wife called?
10. Where is the Ross Sea?
11. Upon which river does Dallas, Texas stand?
12. Upper Volta is the former name of which modern day country?
13. Into what will a leveret grow?
14. What is the unit of currency in Indonesia?
15. Who was the last king of Austria?

Quiz 32 Answers

1. Humerus
2. Colours
3. 1985

4. Robert Browning
5. Eos
6. Boot
7. Beetles
8. Pakistan
9. Wilma
10. Antarctica
11. Trinity
12. Burkina Faso
13. Hare
14. Rupiah
15. Karl

Quiz 33

1. From where was the birdman played by Burt Lancaster?
2. Georgetown is the capital of which country?
3. In the game of Mah-jong how many tiles are there?
4. What was the main cargo of Clipper ships?
5. How many bones are there in the neck of a giraffe?
6. Bysshe was the middle name of which poet?
7. What was the name of Buddy Holly's backing group?
8. Of which island is Douglas the capital?
9. In computer terms, what do the letters ROM stand for?
10. What was Sherpa Tenzing's surname?
11. In the Cinderella story, what was made from a pumpkin?
12. In Greek mythology how many were the number of labours of Hercules?
13. What was the first name of the German car designer Porsche?
14. In the phonetic alphabet, what word represents the letter W?
15. Which pop group did Debbie Harry front?

Quiz 33 Answers

1. Alcatraz
2. Guyana
3. 144
4. Tea
5. 7
6. Percy Shelley
7. Crickets
8. The Isle of Man
9. Read Only Memory
10. Norgay
11. Her coach
12. 12
13. Ferdinand
14. Whisky
15. Blondie

Quiz 34

1. A starfish has how many arms?
2. The Sunshine State is the nickname for which US state?
3. Which is the most westerly city on the African mainland?
4. On August 19th of which year did actor and wit Groucho Marx die?
5. Who performed the James Bond theme for The Man with the Golden Gun?
6. In Greek mythology, which characters have women's faces and bodies but the wings and claws of birds?
7. What is a mistral?
8. Dennis Rodman is associated with which sport?
9. Zagreb is the capital city of which country?
10. By what other name are the Friendly Islands known?
11. The Barber of Seville was composed by whom?
12. A tanner would work with which material?
13. In which African city does the car rally end that begins in Paris?

14. Great Slave Lake is in which country?
15. Which Canadian province lies in between Alberta and Manitoba?

Quiz 34 Answers

1. 5
2. Florida
3. Dakar
4. 1977
5. Lulu
6. Harpies
7. Wind
8. Basketball
9. Croatia
10. Tonga
11. Rossini
12. Leather
13. Dakar
14. Canada
15. Saskatchewan

Quiz 35

1. How many balls are used in a game of billiards?
2. Of what was Aurora the Roman goddess?
3. Santiago is the capital of which country?
4. Of which country is Taipei the capital?
5. Of what is tomophobia the fear?
6. In which movie did Buzz Lightyear first appear?
7. In which chapel are Popes elected?
8. Juventus Football Club play in which city?
9. Brigham who led the Mormons to Utah had what surname?
10. Which chemical element makes up 92.7% of the universe?
11. Britain's Princess Diana was killed in a car accident in Paris on August 31st in which year?

12. What is the name of the world's smallest ocean?
13. Lufthansa is the national airline of which country?
14. What is the real first name of Brad Pitt?
15. Who wrote the novel The Phantom of the Opera?

Quiz 35 Answers

1. 3
2. The dawn
3. Chile
4. Taiwan
5. Surgery
6. Toy Story
7. Sistine chapel
8. Turin
9. Young
10. Hydrogen
11. 1997
12. Arctic
13. Germany
14. William
15. Gaston Leroux

Quiz 36

1. From what type of stone is the Taj Mahal built?
2. What is the official language of Chile?
3. Muskie and Vince assisted which cartoon law enforcer?
4. Oenology is the study of what?
5. Mustard belongs to which vegetable family?
6. Nashville is the capital of which American state?
7. Of what colour is xanthophobia is the fear?
8. Nephology is the scientific study of what?
9. What is the capital city of the US state of Oregon?
10. Including jokers how many cards are there in a standard deck?
11. Into which sea does the Nile flow?
12. Which playing card is known as, the curse of Scotland?

13. What name is given to a female donkey?
14. Tegucigalpa is the capital of which country?
15. Mount McKinley is in which US state?

Quiz 36 Answers

1. Marble
2. Spanish
3. Deputy Dawg
4. Wine
5. Cabbage
6. Tennessee
7. Yellow
8. Clouds
9. Salem
10. 54
11. Mediterranean
12. Nine of diamonds
13. Jenny
14. Honduras
15. Alaska

Quiz 37

1. How many bones form an adult human skull?
2. "All happy families are alike; each unhappy family is unhappy in its own way" is the first line of which novel?
3. Dimanche is the French name for which day?
4. In Shakespeare's play, Romeo and Juliet, what was Juliet's surname?
5. Edward Rochester and Mr Brocklehurst are characters in which novel?
6. How many Great Lakes are there?
7. For what does the D stand for in AIDS?
8. In mythology what was the name of the prophetess who was never believed?
9. From which fruit are prunes made?

10. How many human passengers were aboard Noah's ark?
11. In snooker, how many points is the blue ball worth?
12. What fraction of a circle's diameter is its radius?
13. Of what is pogonophobia the fear?
14. What is the Spanish word for table?
15. What is the name of the string of beads is used in a Catholic prayer?

Quiz 37 Answers

1. 22
2. Anna Karenina
3. Sunday
4. Capulet
5. Jane Eyre
6. 5
7. Deficiency
8. Cassandra
9. Plum
10. 8
11. 5
12. Half
13. Beards
14. Mesa
15. Rosary

Quiz 38

1. "Once there were four children whose names were Peter, Susan, Edmond, and Lucy" is the first line of which novel?
2. How many permanent Members of the Security Council are there?
3. Pediophobia is a fear of what?
4. What is St Vitus the patron saint of?
5. Phnom Penh is the capital city of which country?
6. Pizza is Italian for what word?
7. What is struck in a game of badminton?

8. Primula veris is the Latin name for which plant?
9. Ratabaga is another name for which vegetable?
10. What is South America's highest mountain range?
11. Other than a walrus, what is the only sea creature that possesses an ivory tusk?
12. Pakistan and which other country are linked by the Khyber pass?
13. What is shepherd's purse?
14. Mardi is the French name for which day?
15. Martin Luther King delivered his "I have a dream that one day" speech at The Lincoln Memorial in Washington, DC, on August 28th of which year?

Quiz 38 Answers

1. The Lion, the Witch and the Wardrobe
2. 25
3. Dolls
4. Dancers
5. Cambodia
6. Pie
7. Shuttlecock
8. Cowslip
9. Swede
10. Andes
11. Narwhal
12. Afghanistan
13. Plant
14. Tuesday
15. 1963

Quiz 39

1. Of what is gynaephobia the fear?
2. "Once upon a time and a very good time it was there was a moocow coming along down the road" is the first line of which novel?
3. How many letters are there in the Cambodian alphabet?

4. Belarus is the capital city of which country?
5. On television kind of creature was Flipper?
6. Great Bear is the popular name for which constellation?
7. What is the real first name of actor Mickey Rourke?
8. Where is the volcano Olympus Mons?
9. Ra is the chemical symbol for which element?
10. Rabat is the capital of which Kingdom?
11. Who wrote the poem 'The Owl and the Pussycat'?
12. In 1827, in which US city was the first Mardi Gras celebration held?
13. Which actor played the role of Nelson Mandela in the 2009 movie Invictus?
14. What sort of creature is a skate?
15. The Harlem Globetrotters play what sport?

Quiz 39 Answers

1. Women
2. A Portrait of the Artist as a Young Man
3. 74
4. Minsk
5. Dolphin
6. Ursa Major
7. Philip
8. Mars
9. Radium
10. Morocco
11. Edward Lear
12. New Orleans
13. Morgan Freeman
14. Fish
15. Basketball

Quiz 40

1. Dhaka is the capital of which country?
2. On which river is the city of Hamburg?
3. Oology is the scientific study of what?
4. Oslo is the capital city of which country?
5. Paraguay has borders with Argentina, Brazil and which other country?
6. Quicksilver is another name for which metal?
7. What is the collective noun for rabbits?
8. In 'A Christmas Carol' what was the name of the first ghost to visit Scrooge?
9. Brandy should be served in what sort of glass?
10. What is the coloured part of the eye that surrounds the pupil?
11. Where in 1912 was the newspaper Pravda first published?
12. What was the surname of US aviator Charles, who made the first solo non-stop transatlantic flight?
13. What word can go before tunnel, break and mill?
14. Dix is the French word for which number?
15. Lhasa is the capital of which country?

Quiz 40 Answers

1. Bangladesh
2. Elbe
3. Eggs
4. Norway
5. Bolivia
6. Mercury
7. Nest
8. Marley
9. Balloon
10. Iris
11. Russia
12. Lindbergh
13. Wind

14. Ten
15. Tibet

Quiz 41

1. "One may as well begin with Helen's letters to her sister" is the first line of which novel?
2. Australia country celebrated its bicentenary in which year?
3. How many members does a rowing eights crew have?
4. What is the unit of currency in Lebanon?
5. In legend which knight caused the death of the Lady of Shallott?
6. Switzerland has how many cantons?
7. Lima is the capital city of which South American country?
8. Captain Snort commanded Pippin Fort in which children's television series?
9. A limerick is made up of how many lines?
10. Montserrat is an Island in which West Indian group?
11. Artist Pablo Picasso was what nationality?
12. Leo and Aries are two of the fire signs of the zodiac, which is the third?
13. Mount Everest is located on the border between Tibet and which other country?
14. What is the value of the green ball in snooker?
15. Which actress's husbands included Joe DiMaggio and Arthur Miller?

Quiz 41 Answers

1. Howard's End
2. 1988
3. 9
4. Livre
5. Lancelot
6. 26
7. Peru

8. Camberwick Green
9. 5
10. Leeward Islands
11. Spanish
12. Sagittarius
13. Nepal
14. 3
15. Marilyn Monroe

Quiz 42

1. Holden Caulfield and Jane Gallagher are characters in which novel?
2. Bill Clinton was elected US president, defeating the incumbent George Bush, in which year?
3. The Uffizi Gallery is in what city?
4. On what part of the body are epaulettes worn?
5. On a conventional dartboard how many scoring zones are there?
6. In the television sitcom Friends which character has the middle name Muriel?
7. Olympia is the capital of which US state?
8. In vehicle International identification letters what country is represented by AND?
9. Launched in 1954 what was the name of the world's first nuclear powered submarine?
10. Of what is apiphobia the fear?
11. Nairobi is the capital city of which African country?
12. On which continent is Vincon Massif the highest peak?
13. What ancient unit of measurement is supposedly the distance from the elbow to the tip of the index finger?
14. What are Buff Orpington and Rhode Island Red?
15. In avoirdupois weight what is equivalent to 105 kilograms?

Quiz 42 Answers

1. The Catcher in the Rye
2. 1992
3. Florence
4. Shoulders
5. 82
6. Chandler
7. Washington
8. Andorra
9. Nautilus
10. Bees
11. Kenya
12. Antarctica
13. Cubit
14. Chicken
15. Ton

Quiz 43

1. Tarzan actor Johnny Weissmuller was a medallist in what Olympic event?
2. There are many carats in pure gold?
3. The Canary Islands are named after which animal?
4. In mythology who flew too close to the sun with wax-attached wings and fell into sea and drowned?
5. The character Becky Sharp appeared in which novel?
6. What word means the killing of a king?
7. The art of clipping hedges into various shapes has what name?
8. South Africa surrounds which country?
9. The city of Philadelphia is in which US state?
10. Spain, France and which other country has a Mediterranean and an Atlantic coastline?
11. The 1912 Olympic Games were held in which city?
12. Naturalist Carolus Linnaeus was what nationality?
13. Rockhopper and emperor are types of which bird?
14. Of what is meteorology the scientific study?

15. Singer Elvis Presley was born on January 8th in which year?

Quiz 43 Answers

1. Swimming
2. 24
3. Dog
4. Icarus
5. Vanity Fair
6. Regicide
7. Topiary
8. Lesotho
9. Pennsylvania
10. Morocco
11. Stockholm
12. Swedish
13. Penguin
14. Weather
15. 1935

Quiz 44

1. There are how many letters in the Greek Alphabet?
2. On which part of the body is a tracheotomy performed?
3. What breed of farm animal is a Polwarth?
4. Salvia officinalis is better known as which herb?
5. Samedi is the French word for which day?
6. Austin is the capital of which US state?
7. What brandy is distilled from cider?
8. Reykjavik is the capital city of which country?
9. What is the first letter of the Greek alphabet?
10. Roseau is the capital and chief port of which independent island nation?
11. Sally Bowles is a character in which movie?
12. A cranefly has how many legs?
13. What is the Celsius temperature scale otherwise known as?

14. What can be a puzzle or a woodworking tool?
15. Boxer Holyfield who defeated Mike Tyson in 1996 has what first name?

Quiz 44 Answers

1. 24
2. Throat
3. Sheep
4. Sage
5. Saturday
6. Texas
7. Calvados
8. Iceland
9. Alpha
10. Dominica
11. Cabaret
12. 6
13. Centigrade
14. Jigsaw
15. Evander

Quiz 45

1. The St Valentine's Day Massacre took place in which US city?
2. How many English letters are there in the Hawaiian alphabet?
3. The terms curd and whey are associated with the making of what?
4. On which island is the town of Cagliari?
5. What is the common name for sodium bicarbonate?
6. The Three Musketeers were Athos, Porthos and whom?
7. There are how many events in the heptathlon?
8. The territory of Christmas Island belongs to which country?
9. Of whom is Helen the patron saint?
10. The Sound Of Music is set in which European country?

11. Which lost city of the Incas did Hiram Bingham rediscover in the Peruvian Andes in 1911?
12. What was the name of the character Halle Berry played in the 2002 Bond Movie 'Die Another Day'?
13. Which Louis was the first to cross the English Channel by aeroplane?
14. Dictator Pol Pot ruled which country?
15. What is the currency of the Republic of Ireland?

Quiz 45 Answers

1. Chicago
2. 12
3. Cheese
4. Sardinia
5. Baking Soda
6. Aramis
7. 7
8. Australia
9. Archaeologists
10. Austria
11. Machu Picchu
12. Jinx
13. Bleriot
14. Cambodia
15. Euro

Quiz 46

1. How many ounces are there in an avoirdupois pound?
2. The gharial is a species of which reptile?
3. The Gulf of San Matias is off the coast of which country?
4. Scottish lakes are known by what name?
5. The Hoover Dam in America was built on which river?
6. Sherlock Holmes wore type of hat?
7. The Hundred Years' War was fought between France and which other country?

8. The island of Mauritius is in which ocean?
9. How many musicians are there in a septet?
10. Of which family of birds is the jay a member?
11. Shooting stars are more commonly referred to as what?
12. The Jumna is a tributary of which Indian River?
13. The Kip is the currency of which country?
14. Concord is the capital of which US state?
15. What is the collective term for a group of harpists?

Quiz 46 Answers

1. 16
2. Crocodile
3. Argentina
4. Lochs
5. Colorado
6. Deerstalker
7. England
8. Indian
9. 7
10. Crow
11. Meteors
12. Ganges
13. Laos
14. New Hampshire
15. Melody

Quiz 47

1. Sketós, métrios and glykís are different types of Greek what?
2. How many Nobel prizes are awarded each year?
3. What word means slower than the speed of sound?
4. Which bird lays the world's largest egg?
5. Who was the first woman to fly across the Atlantic?
6. Author Mario who wrote The Godfather has what surname?
7. Where in the human body are the Islets of Langerhans?

8. A shape with eight sides has what name?
9. Which book begins with The Knight's Tale and ends with The Parson's Tale?
10. Who was the Greek God of Time?
11. Sarajevo is the capital of which country?
12. Methyphobia the fear of what?
13. How many court cards are there in a pack of cards?
14. What was the surname of the USSR President who encouraged the policy of Glassnost?
15. In J.R.R. Tolkien's The Lord of the Rings how many rings were given to the Dwarf Lords?

Quiz 47 Answers

1. Coffee
2. 6
3. Subsonic
4. Ostrich
5. Amelia Earhart
6. Puzo
7. Pancreas
8. Octagon
9. The Canterbury Tales
10. Chronos
11. Bosnia
12. Alcohol
13. 12
14. Gorbachov
15. 7

Quiz 48

1. There are how many letters in the Italian alphabet?
2. Which famous bridge spans San Francisco bay?
3. What was the name of the super tanker that ran aground off the Alaskan coast in 1989 spilling crude oil?
4. Which chess piece can only move diagonally?
5. Kenya is bordered by which country to the south?

6. How many masts are there on a clipper sailing ship?
7. What is the name of the record company founded by the Beatles in 1968?
8. Which Chinese dynasty began in AD 618 and ended in 907?
9. Stephen Burton was the birth name of which Hollywood actor?
10. What nationality was the composer Sibelius?
11. The 1956 Olympic Games were held in which city?
12. What is a natterjack?
13. Which flag features 5 rings?
14. N is the symbol for which chemical element?
15. In the phonetic alphabet what word represents the letter G?

Quiz 48 Answers

1. 21
2. Golden Gate
3. Exxon Valdez
4. Bishop
5. Tanzania
6. 3
7. Apple
8. Tang
9. Burt Lancaster
10. Finnish
11. Melbourne
12. Toad
13. Olympic
14. Nitrogen
15. Golf

Quiz 49

1. Which city is known as The Eternal City?
2. How many months have exactly 31 days?
3. Zn is the symbol for which chemical element?
4. Which city is served by the airport coded CDG?
5. The Davis Cup is associated with which sport?
6. How many wooden pins are arranged in a game of skittles?
7. Of what is trypanophobia the fear of?
8. The Indus River rises in which country?
9. A hendecagon has how many sides?
10. Which element has the highest melting point?
11. The first dog in space had what name?
12. Which mythical king turned everything he touched into gold?
13. Bastille Day is celebrated on July 14th in which country?
14. In which country is Ayres Rock?
15. Which explorer discovered the island of Jamaica?

Quiz 49 Answers

1. Rome
2. 7
3. Zinc
4. Paris
5. Tennis
6. 9
7. Injections
8. Tibet
9. 11
10. Carbon
11. Laika
12. Midas
13. France
14. Australia
15. Christopher Columbus

Quiz 50

1. There are how many pockets on a snooker table?
2. What is the Japanese parliament called?
3. What is the largest fresh water lake in North America?
4. Chronomentrophobia is the name given to the fear of what?
5. Who was the author of the James Bond books?
6. Who was the Roman God of Wine?
7. In mathematics, what does the letter L stand for in the abbreviation LCD?
8. The role of Eliza Doolittle in the movie My Fair Lady was played by which actress?
9. What is the fourth letter of the Greek alphabet?
10. Justin Timberlake was formerly a vocalist with which band?
11. Nick Carraway, Daisy Buchannan and Jordan Baker are characters in which novel?
12. Transylvania is in which country?
13. In cricket how many balls are there in an over?
14. In which country are the rivers Vistula and Oder that flow into the Baltic Sea?
15. What is the monetary unit of Thailand?

Quiz 50 Answers

1. 6
2. Diet
3. Superior
4. Clocks
5. Ian Fleming
6. Bacchus
7. Lowest
8. Audrey Hepburn
9. Delta
10. N Sync
11. The Great Gatsby
12. Romania

13. 6
14. Poland
15. Baht

Quiz 51

1. How many inches are there in 2.54 cm?
2. What is the name for the outermost part of the Sun's atmosphere?
3. Logophobia is the fear of what?
4. In Roman Mythology who is the messenger of the gods?
5. In fiction who was Pinocchio's father?
6. In golf the No 10 iron is usually called what?
7. An invertebrate lacks what?
8. What does the C in CIA stand for?
9. In Scrabble, how many points is the letter M worth?
10. How many players are there in a water polo team?
11. What name is given to an angle less than 90°?
12. Li is the symbol for which chemical element?
13. What is the real surname of actor Nicolas Cage?
14. What was the name of the magical land created by C.S. Lewis in a series of books?
15. How many players make up a team in Ice Hockey?

Quiz 51 Answers

1. 1
2. Corona
3. Words
4. Mercury
5. Geppetto
6. Wedge
7. Backbone
8. Central
9. 3
10. 7
11. Acute
12. Lithium

13. Coppola
14. Narnia
15. 6

Quiz 52

1. How many players are there in a hockey team?
2. Wile E Coyote chases which cartoon character?
3. Sana'a is the capital city of which country?
4. In the novel Gulliver's Travels what was Gulliver's first name?
5. Windy City is the nickname of which US city?
6. In the periodic table which element is number 79?
7. With which country did Tanganyika merge to form Tanzania?
8. Scottish blackface and cheviot are breeds of which animal?
9. In Herman Melville's novel 'Moby Dick' what is the name of the boat?
10. What does a tegestologist collect?
11. In legend what was the name of King Arthur's sword?
12. Anthropophobia the fear of what?
13. What is Brazil's national language?
14. In golf what name is given to 2 under par for a hole?
15. Santa Fe is the capital of which US state?

Quiz 52 Answers

1. 11
2. Roadrunner
3. Yemen
4. Lemuel
5. Chicago
6. Gold
7. Zanzibar
8. Sheep
9. Pequod
10. Beer mats

11. Excalibur
12. People
13. Portuguese
14. Eagle
15. New Mexico

Quiz 53

1. What is the collective noun for a group of owls?
2. In Greek mythology who was the god of wine?
3. What is the 'perfect score' in a game of Ten Pin Bowling?
4. Tehran is the capital city of which country?
5. Who at the age of 17 became the fifth emperor of Rome?
6. What is the Spanish word for ten?
7. The Ugly Duckling was written by which author?
8. Who would wear a tutu?
9. How many players are on court during a volleyball game?
10. What name is given to a fork's prong?
11. Cynophobia is the fear of what?
12. In the comic strip what is the name of Dennis the Menace's dog?
13. In Scrabble, how many points is the letter H worth?
14. How many syllables are there in a haiku?
15. What is the world's largest turtle?

Quiz 53 Answers

1. Parliament
2. Dionysus
3. 300
4. Iran
5. Nero
6. Diez
7. Hans Christian Andersen
8. Ballerina

9. 12
10. Tine
11. Dogs
12. Gnasher
13. 4
14. 17
15. Leatherback

Quiz 54

1. How many players are there in an American football team?
2. In Roman mythology who was the goddess of fruits?
3. In rugby union how many points are scored for a try?
4. Lait is the French word for what?
5. What is the Haitian unit of currency?
6. Baton Rouge is the capital of which US state?
7. What is the chemical symbol for Plutonium?
8. Who wrote the poem: The Rime of the Ancient Mariner?
9. In amateur boxing how many rounds make up a bout?
10. Trichophobia is the fear of what?
11. Jafar was the villain in which Disney movie?
12. Of what is arachnophobia the fear?
13. How many stars are on the European Union flag?
14. What name is given to the line on ships that indicates the maximum loading permitted?
15. Columbus is the capital of which US state?

Quiz 54 Answers

1. 11
2. Pomona
3. 5
4. Milk
5. Gourde
6. Louisiana
7. Pu

8. Samuel Taylor Coleridge
9. 4
10. Hair
11. Aladdin
12. Spiders
13. 12
14. Plimsoll
15. Ohio

Quiz 55

1. A trapezium has how many sides?
2. In mythology who was the sorceress daughter of the King of Colchis?
3. Cartoon character Mr Magoo had what first name?
4. In the human body how is the trachea better known?
5. Frère is the French word for what?
6. Central America consists of how many different countries?
7. In what sport do players take long and short corners?
8. What is written on a staff or stave?
9. How many points does X score in Scrabble?
10. In the Jerome K. Jerome story how many men were in the boat?
11. What is the collective noun for a group of kangaroos?
12. In the U.S.A., what is celebrated on February 2nd and is also the title of a movie?
13. The Atacama Desert is in which country?
14. In the phonetic alphabet, what word represents the letter N?
15. In total how many men have walked on the Moon?

Quiz 55 Answers

1. 4
2. Medea
3. Quincy
4. Windpipe

5. Brother
6. 8
7. Hockey
8. Music
9. 8
10. 3
11. Mob
12. Groundhog Day
13. Chile
14. November
15. 12

Quiz 56

1. Frank who developed Meccano had what surname?
2. A dodecagon has how many sides?
3. In mythology, who was leader of the Argonauts?
4. What is the state capital of New York?
5. In Scrabble, how many points is the letter U worth?
6. Fashion designer Karl, who was born in Hamburg in 1938, has what surname?
7. What is the study of heredity called?
8. Triton is a moon of which planet?
9. Vilnius is the capital of which Baltic republic?
10. W A Mozart airport serves which city?
11. Welsh, Scottish and Irish are what type of dog breed?
12. What country lies immediately to the south of Belarus?
13. Rioja wines are produced in which country?
14. What creature is a Flemish giant?
15. How many different colours are used to make a set of snooker balls?

Quiz 56 Answers

1. Hornby
2. 12
3. Jason
4. Albany
5. 1
6. Lagerfeld
7. Genetics
8. Neptune
9. Lithuania
10. Salzburg
11. Terrier
12. Ukraine
13. Spain
14. Rabbit
15. 8

Quiz 57

1. How many spikes are there in the crown of the Statue of Liberty?
2. The river Yangtze is in which country?
3. In the 2004 movie Troy what is the name of the character played by Brad Pitt?
4. In the phonetic alphabet, what word represents the letter Y?
5. The Algarve is in which country?
6. To which animals does bovine refer?
7. In mythology who was Cupid's earthly love?
8. How many provinces does Canada have?
9. What is the smallest nation in Africa?
10. Atlanta is the capital of which US state?
11. What is the collective noun for a group of bees?
12. The song Don't Cry For Me, Argentina features in which musical?
13. What is measured in hertz?
14. Nyctophobia is the fear of what?

15. How many points are needed to win a game of cribbage?

Quiz 57 Answers

1. 13
2. China
3. Achilles
4. Yankee
5. Portugal
6. Cattle
7. Psyche
8. 10
9. Gambia
10. Georgia
11. Swarm
12. Evita
13. Frequency
14. Darkness
15. 121

Quiz 58

1. How many syllables are there in a monosyllabic word?
2. The city of Bruges is in which country?
3. Las Vegas is in which US state?
4. In what year was Mahatma Gandhi assassinated?
5. What is polytetrafluoroethylene more commonly called?
6. Havana is the capital city of which country?
7. What is the only fruit that grows its seeds on the outside?
8. How many stripes are there on the flag of the United States of America?
9. The novel Tristram Shandy was written by which author?
10. The okapi is a member of which animal family?

11. In the movie All The Presidents Men, Robert Redford and Dustin Hoffman played journalists investigating which break-in?
12. Of what is George the patron saint?
13. Noctiphobia is the fear of what?
14. George, who invented the Kodak box camera, had what surname?
15. Astronomer was Galileo what nationality?

Quiz 58 Answers

1. 1
2. Belgium
3. Nevada
4. 1948
5. Teflon
6. Cuba
7. Strawberry
8. 13
9. Laurence Sterne
10. Giraffe
11. Watergate
12. England
13. Night
14. Eastman
15. Italian

Quiz 59

1. How many territories does Canada have?
2. In Greek mythology who was the winged goddess of victory?
3. Stromboli was a villain in which Disney movie?
4. Fort Knox is in which American state?
5. Of what is ombrophobia the fear?
6. How many pairs of chromosomes in the human body are there in the human body?

7. Split and Zadar are two major cities in which region of Croatia?
8. Swiss mechanical engineer George De Mestrel invented what in the 1940s?
9. How many yards are there in a chain?
10. In Greek mythology, who was the twin brother of Pollux?
11. The Hekla volcano is in which country?
12. Of what is trichology the study?
13. An ornithologist is interested in what?
14. How old was actor and comedian Bob Hope when he died in 2003?
15. What is the currency of Germany?

Quiz 59 Answers

1. 3
2. Nike
3. Pinocchio
4. Kentucky
5. Rain
6. 23
7. Dalmatia
8. Velcro
9. 22
10. Castor
11. Iceland
12. Hair
13. Birds
14. 100
15. Euro

Quiz 60

1. How many players are there in a lacrosse team?
2. The Rialto Bridge is in which city?
3. In mythology what was the name of the female monster with a head of lion, body of goat and tail of a serpent?
4. Of which country is Tripoli the capital?
5. The cerebrum is found in which organ of the body?
6. In music how crotchets are there in a minim?
7. The dog the Shih Tzu was first bred in which country?
8. The eruption of Mount Vesuvius destroyed the city of Pompeii and which other city?
9. The Lek is the unit of currency of which country?
10. The name of which capital city means 'new flower'?
11. How many stomachs does a cow have?
12. The novel Ivanhoe by written by which author?
13. What are elephants called in the Winnie the Pooh books?
14. Which actor played the lead role in the 2009 movie Harry Brown?
15. To whom was Sean Penn married between 1985 and 1989?

Quiz 60 Answers

1. 12
2. Venice
3. Chimera
4. Libya
5. Brain
6. 2
7. Tibet
8. Herculaneum
9. Albania
10. Addis Ababa
11. 4
12. Sir Walter Scott
13. Heffalumps

14. Michael Caine
15. Madonna

Quiz 61

1. How many vertebrae does a human have?
2. The wine Vinho Verdi is produced in which country?
3. To which religion is the river Ganges sacred?
4. The port of Lagos is in which country?
5. In the television series what is the name of Homer Simpson's bowling team?
6. The people of Mexico speak which language?
7. In blackjack, the Ten, Jack, Queen and King are each worth how many points?
8. The 1996 Olympic Games were held in which city?
9. In which language do the letters omega, pi and lambda appear?
10. Madison is the capital of which US state?
11. The deathcap is the most poisonous type of what?
12. Tokelau is a dependency of which country?
13. Which television soap is set in a suburb of Melbourne?
14. In computing how many bits are there in a byte?
15. A dog called Laika become the first space traveller in which year?

Quiz 61 Answers

1. 34
2. Portugal
3. Hindu
4. Nigeria
5. Pin Pals
6. Spanish
7. 10
8. Atlanta
9. Greek
10. Wisconsin
11. Mushroom

12. New Zealand
13. Neighbours
14. 8
15. 1957

Quiz 62

1. Des Moines is the capital of which US state?
2. In what year did the first successful Mars landings take place?
3. Lake Disappointment is in which country?
4. In mythology who was the son of Aphrodite?
5. What bird is the symbol of the USA?
6. In which television series did the characters Little Joe, Hoss and Ben Cartwright appear?
7. S is the symbol for which chemical element?
8. Tirana is the capital of what country?
9. To what family of birds does the blackcap belong?
10. In William Shakespeare's "Romeo and Juliet" what is Romeo's last name?
11. Ulan Bator is the capital of which nation?
12. What animal is the ram the male and ewe the female?
13. The Bismarck Archipelago is in which ocean?
14. How many points are there on a sheriff's badge?
15. What creature is sometimes called an eft?

Quiz 62 Answers

1. Iowa
2. 1976
3. Australia
4. Eros
5. Eagle
6. Bonanza
7. Sulphur
8. Albania
9. Warbler
10. Montague

11. Mongolia
12. Sheep
13. Pacific
14. 7
15. Newt

Quiz 63

1. Denver is the capital of which US state?
2. Staten Island is in which city?
3. The pineal gland is in which organ of the body?
4. In mythology how many Gorgons were there?
5. The town of Tequila is in which country?
6. Trinidad lies off the coast of which South American country?
7. What are the discs between the bones of the spine made of?
8. In which Asian country did the Long March of the 1930s take place?
9. A vintner deals in what?
10. What does the Hungarian word paprika mean?
11. In which novel do the characters Meg, Jo, Beth and Amy appear?
12. What bird lays its eggs in the nests of other birds?
13. In which year did the Second World War end?
14. What boxing weight category comes between bantamweight and lightweight?
15. In the musical Annie, what is orphan Annie's dog called?

Quiz 63 Answers

1. Colorado
2. New York
3. Brain
4. 3
5. Mexico
6. Venezuela
7. Cartilage

8. China
9. Wine
10. Pepper
11. Little Women
12. Cuckoo
13. 1945
14. Featherweight
15. Sandy

Quiz 64

1. Dover is the capital of which US state?
2. In computing how many megabytes are in a gigabyte?
3. The Roman god Mars was god of what?
4. Sicily is the capital of which country?
5. The Alhambra Palace is in which European country?
6. Of which European country is Joseph the patron saint?
7. San Quentin prison is in which US state?
8. The disease caused by lack of vitamin C has what name?
9. What bird is known at the 'butcher's bird'?
10. The mummies of Egyptian Pharaohs were often buried in what type of transport, believed to assist them to travel to the next world?
11. What are the smallest blood vessels in the body called?
12. What can be cantilever or pontoon?
13. Memphis was once the capital of which country?
14. How many basic "pillars" of Islam are there?
15. In the board game Cluedo how many characters are there?

Quiz 64 Answers

1. Delaware
2. 1024
3. War
4. Palermo
5. Spain

6. Belgium
7. California
8. Scurvy
9. Shrike
10. Boats
11. Capillaries
12. Bridges
13. Egypt
14. 5
15. 6

Quiz 65

1. The Gulf of Ob is in which ocean?
2. Who is the Roman goddess of the hunt and moon?
3. In the game of draughts, how many men does a player start with?
4. Who wrote the poem The Rolling English Road?
5. Which vegetables can be French, runner or baked?
6. Of what is odontophobia the fear?
7. Montgomery is the capital of which US state?
8. What is God called by members of the Islamic or Muslim faith?
9. Which white-berried parasite grows on apple trees?
10. In the movie Casablanca was the name of the pianist?
11. Which Walter founded the US state of Virginia?
12. Nicosia is the capital of which country?
13. In which year did the board game Scrabble make its debut?
14. Na is the symbol for which chemical element?
15. The flowers of the saffron are what colour?

Quiz 65 Answers

1. Artic
2. Diana
3. 12
4. G. K. Chesterton

5. Beans
6. Teeth
7. Alabama
8. Allah
9. Mistletoe
10. Sam
11. Raleigh
12. Cyprus
13. 1955
14. Sodium
15. Purple

Quiz 66

1. What colour are the flowers of the lily of the valley?
2. The Empire State is the nickname for which US state?
3. What currency is used in South Africa?
4. The cartoon family the Simpsons live in which town?
5. What is the birthstone for September?
6. Of which country is the Dalai Lama spiritual leader?
7. What is a baby goat called?
8. The city of Mecca is in which country?
9. A curved stick called a caman is used in which game?
10. Who wrote the play The Glass Menagerie?
11. In which African country is Timbuktu?
12. The song "you'll never walk alone" comes from which musical?
13. C is the chemical symbol for which element?
14. On a roulette wheel what is the highest number?
15. Who was the first to fly solo around the world in a hot air balloon?

Quiz 66 Answers

1. White
2. New York
3. Rand
4. Springfield

5. Sapphire
6. Tibet
7. Kid
8. Saudi Arabia
9. Shinty
10. Tennessee Williams
11. Mali
12. Carousel
13. Carbon
14. 36
15. Steve Fossett

Quiz 67

1. In the musical The Wizard of Oz where is Dorothy from?
2. Which is the third major planet from the sun?
3. The state of Punjab is in which Asian nation?
4. In which palace does the French President live?
5. Of Mice and Men was written by which author?
6. In which borough of New York is Wall Street?
7. Fromage is the French word for what?
8. What do cartographers make?
9. Co is the chemical symbol for which element?
10. What is a Portuguese man-o-war?
11. Anemone is another name for which flower?
12. What is the name for a female ferret?
13. The island of Nauru is in which ocean?
14. What is the collective noun for a group of apes?
15. Which drink is named after Jerez in Spain?

Quiz 67 Answers

1. Kansas
2. Earth
3. India
4. Elysée

5. John Steinbeck
6. Manhattan
7. Cheese
8. Maps
9. Cobalt
10. Jellyfish
11. Windflower
12. Gill
13. Pacific
14. Shrewdness
15. Sherry

Quiz 68

1. Gaul was the Roman name for which country?
2. Hawaii became the 50th state of the United States of America in which year?
3. A fletcher makes what?
4. The Sargasso Sea is in which ocean?
5. Who wrote Finnegan's Wake?
6. The remains of Carthage are in which present day city?
7. What is a common spadefoot?
8. What is the collective name for a set of bells?
9. How is 'Hedera helix' better known?
10. Montpelier is the capital of which US state?
11. What is 'Buzz' Aldrin's real first name?
12. The Sabin vaccine is used to prevent which disease?
13. In which year did Israel become a nation state?
14. A deficiency of iron in the body causes what?
15. What is the medical name for the breastbone?

Quiz 68 Answers

1. France
2. 1959
3. Arrows
4. Atlantic
5. James Joyce

6. Tunis
7. Toad
8. Peal
9. Ivy
10. Vermont
11. Edwin
12. Polio
13. 1948
14. Anaemia
15. Sternum

Quiz 69

1. The port of Bergen is in which European country?
2. What colour submarine did the Beatles sing about?
3. The Roman numeral L stands for which number?
4. The Euro replaced which currency in Austria?
5. What is a noctule?
6. What type of Italian bread is made with olive oil?
7. Of what is acrophobia the fear?
8. What constellation depicts a hunter with club and shield?
9. Beurre is the French word for what?
10. What did Edmund Halley invent in 1717?
11. Doce is the Spanish word for which number?
12. What is the smallest two-digit prime number?
13. Which is the softest form of calcium carbonate?
14. Who wrote the novel Utopia?
15. A drey is the home of which animal?

Quiz 69 Answers

1. Norway
2. Yellow
3. 50
4. Schilling
5. Bat
6. Ciabatta

7. Heights
8. Orion
9. Butter
10. Diving Bell
11. Twelve
12. 11
13. Chalk
14. Sir Thomas More
15. Squirrel

Quiz 70

1. What currency is used in Brazil?
2. In Peter Pan what did the crocodile swallow?
3. A Geiger counter detects what?
4. What is the collective noun for a group of hedgehogs?
5. Who was the Roman God of Time?
6. Cardiology is the scientific study of what?
7. Plume is the French word for what?
8. What connects Gold, Sword, Juno, Omaha and Utah?
9. Grimaldi is the surname of which European principality's ruling family?
10. What is the collective noun for a group of peacocks?
11. In which of the arts would you see a pas de deux?
12. In the novel Treasure Island what is the name of Long John Silver's parrot?
13. What is the total number of spots on a die?
14. Aer Lingus is the national airline of which country?
15. What is the state capital of South Australia?

Quiz 70 Answers

1. Real
2. Alarm clock
3. Radiation
4. Array
5. Saturn
6. The heart

7. Pen
8. D Day
9. Monaco
10. Muster
11. Ballet
12. Captain Flint
13. 21
14. Republic of Ireland
15. Adelaide

Quiz 71

1. The Galapagos Islands belong to which country?
2. What game starts with a squidge off?
3. A camel with two humps is called what?
4. What does the musical term forte mean?
5. How is the Chilean pine tree commonly known?
6. H the chemical symbol for what element?
7. Caribou is another name what animal?
8. What is a person who carries out the instructions of a will called?
9. Yabba dabba do is the catchphrase of which cartoon character?
10. How is deoxyribonucleic acid better known?
11. Which poet wrote Daffodils?
12. Of what was Vulcan the Roman God?
13. What device does a musician use to pluck strings?
14. In the Dirty Harry movies what make of gun did Clint Eastwood use?
15. Topeka is the capital city of which US state?

Quiz 71 Answers

1. Ecuador
2. Tiddlywinks
3. Bactrian
4. Loud
5. Monkey Puzzle

6. Hydrogen
7. Reindeer
8. Executor
9. Fred Flintstone
10. DNA
11. William Wordsworth
12. Fire
13. Plectrum
14. Magnum
15. Kansas

Quiz 72

1. A saluki is what type of creature?
2. F represents which element on the periodic table?
3. What can be workers or drones?
4. Stanley is the capital of which islands?
5. What is the unit of currency is Yemen?
6. Dendrophobia is the fear of what?
7. A horologist is the expert maker of what?
8. Who was the Greek goddess of love and beauty?
9. "I think, therefore I am" was said by whom?
10. What flavour is the Greek spirit Ouzo?
11. Marsh gas is an alternate name for which gas?
12. What is an angle greater than 180° called?
13. The Last Supper was painted by which artist?
14. What is the largest island in the Mediterranean Sea?
15. Cerumen is the medical term for what?

Quiz 72 Answers

1. Dog
2. Fluorine
3. Bees
4. Falklands
5. Rial
6. Trees
7. Clocks

8. Aphrodite
9. Descartes
10. Aniseed
11. Methane
12. Reflex
13. Leonardo Da Vinci
14. Sicily
15. Earwax

Quiz 73

1. What is found in a skein or a gaggle?
2. Photophobia the fear of what?
3. What is couscous made from?
4. Ni is the chemical symbol for which element?
5. In which country would you kiss the Blarney Stone?
6. What is the length in yards of a cricket pitch?
7. Maid Marian was the girlfriend of whom?
8. What is a scallion?
9. The male reproductive organ of a plant has what name?
10. What is the first odd prime number?
11. Saltpetre is another name for what?
12. What is the unit of currency in Honduras?
13. The Japanese art of flower arranging is called what?
14. On Sesame Street what is the name of the Grouch?
15. What does the Venus de Milo lack?

Quiz 73 Answers

1. Geese
2. Light
3. Semolina
4. Nickel
5. Ireland
6. 22
7. Robin Hood
8. Onion
9. Stamen

10. 3
11. Potassium nitrate
12. Lempira
13. Ikebana
14. Oscar
15. Arms

Quiz 74

1. Aubergine is an alternative name for what?
2. What is an alewife?
3. 12 is the atomic number for what?
4. A communal settlement in Israel is called what?
5. What is a mature male horse called?
6. A female deer is called what?
7. What is the basic unit of currency in Jordan?
8. Flora is the Roman Goddess of what?
9. The Latin word aqua means what?
10. What does the W stand for in former US president George W Bush's name?
11. An angle that measures between 90 and 180 degrees is called what?
12. What is the collective noun for a group of monkeys?
13. The claw of a bird of prey is called what?
14. What is the collective noun for a group of racehorses?
15. Which artist painted The Laughing Cavalier?

Quiz 74 Answers

1. The eggplant
2. Fish
3. Silicon
4. Kibbutz
5. Stallion
6. Doe
7. Dinar
8. Flowers
9. Water

10. Walker
11. Obtuse
12. Troop
13. Talon
14. String
15. Frans Hals

Quiz 75

1. What is the currency of Luxembourg?
2. Paul McCartney's fashion designer daughter has what first name?
3. What sort of material is ebony?
4. Shannon is the longest river in which country?
5. What is the most western state of the USA?
6. Anemophobia is the fear of what?
7. What is the world's only poisonous bird?
8. In The Jungle Book what is the name of the tiger?
9. Satchmo was the nickname of whom?
10. What is the name of the long-haired ox native to Tibet?
11. The Roman numeral D stands for which number?
12. What type of fruit is a jargonelle?
13. Who is the Roman god of the sea?
14. English scientist Faraday had what first name?
15. What is the official language of Egypt?

Quiz 75 Answers

1. Euro
2. Stella
3. Wood
4. Ireland
5. Alaska
6. Wind
7. Pitohui
8. Shere Khan
9. Louis Armstrong
10. Yak

11. 500
12. Pear
13. Neptune
14. Michael
15. Arabic

Quiz 76

1. What is the Fahrenheit equivalent of 10 degrees centigrade?
2. Osteology is the scientific study of what?
3. Eau is the French word for what?
4. What is the Ghanaian unit of currency?
5. El Al is the national airline of which country?
6. Luanda is the capital of which country?
7. What is the second largest desert in the world?
8. In the TV series "Daktari" what was the name of the cross-eyed lion?
9. What is the main ingredient of hummus?
10. In the Bible who killed the giant Goliath?
11. Who composed the music for South Pacific?
12. Artist Magritte was what nationality?
13. What is the Latin translation of "I came, I saw, I conquered"?
14. Sackbut the former name of which musical instrument?
15. What name is given to a young kangaroo?

Quiz 76 Answers

1. 50
2. Bones
3. Water
4. Cedi
5. Israel
6. Angola
7. Gobi
8. Clarence
9. Chickpeas

10. David
11. Richard Rogers
12. Belgian
13. Veni, vidi, vici
14. Trombone
15. Joey

Quiz 77

1. What is added to milk to make porridge?
2. Qantas is the name of which country's national airline?
3. Who was the narrator of the stories of The One Thousand and One Nights?
4. What is the collective noun for a group of toads?
5. On a map what is the name of a line that joins places of equal height?
6. What is the currency of South Korea?
7. Scapula is the medical name for what?
8. A beagle is what type of creature?
9. What is the name of Charles Schulz's most famous cartoon strip?
10. The marsh marigold is another name for which flower?
11. What is the highest mountain in New Zealand?
12. Leo Baekeland invented which commercial plastic?
13. What is the name for the scientific study of word origins?
14. In which city would you travel in a gondola?
15. What is the largest island in the Caribbean?

Quiz 77 Answers

1. Oats
2. Australia
3. Scheherazade
4. Knot
5. Contour
6. Won
7. The shoulder blade

8. Dog
9. Peanuts
10. Kingcup
11. Cook
12. Bakelite
13. Etymology
14. Venice
15. Cuba

Quiz 78

1. What is the brightest star in the northern hemisphere?
2. Edelweiss is the national flower of which country?
3. Who was the Roman god of woods and fields?
4. What is the currency of Madagascar?
5. Composer Scott, who wrote the music The Entertainer, had what surname?
6. At the Battle of Rorke's Drift who did the English fight?
7. What is actor Bruce Willis's real first name?
8. A kookaburra is what kind of bird?
9. What is the first sign of the zodiac?
10. Monophobia is the fear of what?
11. What is the highest non-infinite termed number?
12. On a dartboard what number is opposite 20?
13. A lotus flower is the national symbol of which country?
14. Who composed The Firebird?
15. The movie My Friend Flicka starred what type of animal?

Quiz 78 Answers

1. Sirius
2. Austria
3. Silvanus
4. Ariary
5. Joplin
6. Zulus

7. Walter
8. Kingfisher
9. Aries
10. Being alone
11. Googolplex
12. 3
13. India
14. Stravinsky
15. Horse

Quiz 79

1. What is ornamental work in silver or gold thread called?
2. Author Tom who wrote the novel The Bonfire of the Vanities, has what surname?
3. Who was the first Roman Emperor?
4. The ceiling of the Sistine Chapel was painted by whom?
5. What is the only anagram of the word English?
6. In which country would you drive on an Autostrada?
7. What name is given to the fear of moths and butterflies?
8. The Lone Star State is the nickname of which US state?
9. What name is given to the study of the environment?
10. What is the currency of the Seychelles?
11. Mel Gibson played what role in Braveheart?
12. Jennifer Aniston played which character in the TV series Friends?
13. Istanbul was called what while under Greek rule?
14. Composer Debussy has what first name?
15. What is the boiling point of water in degrees Fahrenheit?

Quiz 79 Answers

1. Filigree
2. Wolfe
3. Augustus

4. Michelangelo
5. Shingle
6. Italy
7. Mottephobia
8. Texas
9. Ecology
10. Rupee
11. William Wallace
12. Rachel
13. Byzantium
14. Claude
15. 212

Quiz 80

1. What is the currency unit in Vietnam?
2. A female pig is called what?
3. Which of the Great Lakes in North America has the same name as a U.S. state?
4. The zodiac sign Leo is represented by which animal?
5. What is the longest river in the world?
6. The 1960 Summer Olympics were held in which city?
7. Cologne is on which river?
8. What is the Japanese culinary term for deep fried vegetables?
9. In Greek mythology which creature was half-human and half-horse?
10. Riyadh is the capital city of which country?
11. What number does the Roman numeral V stand for?
12. Paul McCartney's late wife Linda had what maiden name?
13. What is the minimum number of games needed to win a set of tennis?
14. A bandy-bandy is what type of creature?
15. What is the common internet term for junk e-mail?

Quiz 80 Answers

1. Dong
2. Sow
3. Michigan
4. Lion
5. Nile
6. Rome
7. Rhine
8. Tempura
9. Centaur
10. Saudi Arabia
11. 5
12. Eastman
13. 6
14. Snake
15. Spam

Quiz 81

1. What is the hardest substance in the human body?
2. A lodge is the home of which animal?
3. A creature that is active at night and sleeps during the daytime is given what name?
4. What is the unit of currency in Kuwait?
5. The title character in the 1976 movie Carrie was played by which actress?
6. What is the main ingredient of an Italian risotto?
7. In West Side Story who were the Jets rivals?
8. Which US state is immediately south of South Dakota?
9. What is the name given to a triangle where all sides are of different lengths and all angles of different size?
10. Which army rank is the equivalent to the Navy's Lieutenant Commander?
11. The bed of a snooker table is made from what material?
12. Actor Steve McQueen had what real first name?
13. The author of the 1955 novel Lolita had what surname?
14. Which peninsula is home to Spain and Portugal?

15. What is the traditional Christmas flower?

Quiz 81 Answers

1. Enamel
2. Beaver
3. Nocturnal
4. Dinar
5. Sissy Spacek
6. Rice
7. Sharks
8. Nebraska
9. Scalene
10. Major
11. Slate
12. Terence
13. Nabokov
14. Iberian
15. Poinsettia

Quiz 82

1. What is the only fish to have a prehensile tail?
2. In Jules Verne's novel 20,000 Leagues under the Sea what was the name of Captain Nemo's submarine?
3. What is the only US state which borders with just one other?
4. Ho Chi Minh City was the former name of which city?
5. Amnesia is the loss of what?
6. What fruit has a red leathery rind and seeds coated with edible pulp?
7. Pretoria is the administrative capital of which country?
8. Drat and double drat" is the catchphrase of which cartoon character?
9. Which type of lorry is named after a Hindu god?
10. Suicide is Painless was the theme song of which television series?

11. Who was the favourite daughter of Shakespeare's King Lear?
12. What is the country in the United Nations whose name begins with O?
13. A tarantula hawk is what type of creature?
14. The English village of Cerne Abbas is famous for what chalk figure?
15. Who directed and starred in the movie "The Little Tramp"?

Quiz 82 Answers

1. Seahorse
2. Nautilus
3. Maine
4. Saigon
5. Memory
6. Pomegranate
7. South Africa
8. Dick Dastardly
9. Juggernaut
10. M*A*S*H*
11. Cordelia
12. Oman
13. Wasp
14. Giant
15. Charlie Chaplin

Quiz 83

1. Webster, who published a dictionary that is still in use today, had what first name?
2. What is the scientific study of insects called?
3. In a standard Scrabble set what is the total number of tiles?
4. Which steak dish is served uncooked?
5. Diana Prince turns into which super-hero?
6. Buddy Holly had what real first name?

7. What name is given to the Maori ceremonial war dance?
8. Cinco is Spanish for what number?
9. What is the only bone in the human body that is not attached to any other bone?
10. What name is given to the fear of ice or frost?
11. For which movie did Sandra Bullock win the 2010 Academy Award for Best Actress?
12. Nelson, the British Admiral who defeated the French at the battle of Trafalgar had what first name?
13. What is it that makes soda water fizz?
14. Who is the patron saint of children?
15. Burma was the former name which country?

Quiz 83 Answers

1. Noah
2. Entomology
3. 100
4. Steak Tartare
5. Wonder Woman
6. Charles
7. Haka
8. 5
9. Hyoid
10. Pagophobia
11. The Blind Side
12. Horatio
13. Carbon Dioxide
14. Nicholas
15. Myanmar

Quiz 84

1. What is the most abundant metal in the earth's crust?
2. Author Emil, who wrote J'Accuse and Thérèsa Raquin, had what surname?
3. The three-dimensional image created by laser beams is called what?
4. What is the name of the largest lake in South America?
5. In physics what term did Frederick Soddy coin?
6. Where in the human body are the metatarsals?
7. What vegetable has a name that means 'eat all'?
8. Painter Vermeer was what nationality?
9. The Heart of Dixie is the nickname of which US State?
10. 'Ladybird' was the name of which US First Lady?
11. Ermine is the winter coat of which animal?
12. What is the only even prime number?
13. Chlorine element combines with which to make common salt?
14. Until 2006 which was the smallest planet?
15. The shekel is the currency of which country?

Quiz 84 Answers

1. Aluminium
2. Zola
3. Hologram
4. Titicaca
5. Isotope
6. Feet
7. Mange Tout
8. Dutch
9. Alabama
10. Johnson
11. Stoat
12. 2
13. Sodium
14. Pluto
15. Israel

Quiz 85

1. What is the name of The Muppet's frog?
2. Pathology is the medical term for the study of what?
3. In George Orwell's '1984' what is the name of the main character?
4. What was the name of the Wright Brothers' record-setting aircraft?
5. In the Alien series of movies what was the name of the character Sigourney Weaver played?
6. Who shouted "eureka" over what he had discovered in the bath?
7. What is the name of the third longest river in Africa?
8. In which city were the first modern Olympic Games held?
9. Who assassinated US president John F Kennedy?
10. Linus, the inventor of the cylinder lock had what surname?
11. What term is used to describe fertile land being 'rested' for a season?
12. Cheyenne is the capital of which US state?
13. Which actor was the star of "Cocktail"?
14. The role of Mr White in the 1992 movie Reservoir Dogs was played by which actor?
15. What was the name of the Portuguese currency replaced by the Euro?

Quiz 85 Answers

1. Kermit
2. Diseases
3. Winston
4. Flyer
5. Ripley
6. Archimedes
7. Niger
8. Athens
9. Lee Harvey Oswald

10. Yale
11. Fallow
12. Wyoming
13. Tom Cruise
14. Harvey Keitel
15. Escudo

Quiz 86

1. What is the largest inland sea in the world?
2. Spain is separated from France by which range of mountains?
3. Johann Strauss described which river as blue?
4. What is the Italian dish 'zuppa inglese'?
5. Which river flows though Vienna, Bratislava and Belgrade?
6. The character the Scarlet Pimpernel was created by which author?
7. Which type of skiing includes ski jumping and cross-country?
8. The left-side even-numbered page of a book has what name?
9. Actress Sigourney Weaver has what real first name?
10. What is the largest land-locked country in Africa?
11. The Roman symbol C has what value?
12. Matthew, the first man to swim the English Channel had what surname?
13. The Romanovs was the last ruling dynasty of which country?
14. What is the name for a ship's kitchen?
15. The Faeroe Islands are ruled by which country?

Quiz 86 Answers

1. Caspian
2. Pyrenees
3. Danube
4. Trifle
5. Danube

6. Baroness Orczy
7. Nordic
8. Verso
9. Susan
10. Chad
11. 100
12. Webb
13. Russia
14. Galley
15. Denmark

Quiz 87

1. Who was the first European to round the Cape of Good Hope?
2. Spaghetti is what type of food?
3. What is the right-hand side of a ship called?
4. The Euro replaced which currency in Greece in 2002?
5. Goldeneye was the Jamaican home if which author?
6. Lynn Frederick and Britt Ekland were wives of which late actor?
7. Breakfast at Tiffany's was written by which author?
8. What is the name of the strait between Alaska and Siberia?
9. In the movie The Wizard of Oz what was the name of the dog?
10. On July 18th 1955 which amusement park opened in Anaheim, California?
11. What name is given to the Japanese art of paper folding?
12. A painted lady is what type of creature?
13. Which African country is the largest in area?
14. Racing driver Juan-Manuel Fangio was what nationally?
15. What is the only river which flows both north and south of the equator?

Quiz 87 Answers

1. Bartholomew Diaz
2. Pasta
3. Starboard
4. Drachma
5. Ian Fleming
6. Peter Sellers
7. Truman Capote
8. Bering
9. Toto
10. Disneyland
11. Origami
12. Butterfly
13. Sudan
14. Argentinean
15. Congo

Quiz 88

1. What term describes the fineness of yarn?
2. German motor manufacturer Daimler had what first name?
3. In the human body which fluid is stored in the gall bladder?
4. What name is given to the punctuation mark with a dot directly above a comma?
5. A 6 inch net is used in which game?
6. What name is given to animals that feed only on plants?
7. The symbol K represents which chemical element?
8. The vibrissae is what part of a cat?
9. What is the surname of the brothers in the band The Bee Gees?
10. Which creature is composed of 95 per cent water and has no heart, no brain and no blood?
11. Greenland is owned by which country?
12. Which Formula One Grand Prix takes place at Interlagos?
13. The cheese Gaperon is produced in which country?

14. The late US president Ronald Reagan's first lady had what first name?
15. What name is given to a black and white horse?

Quiz 89 Answers

1. Denier
2. Gottlieb
3. Bile
4. Semi-colon
5. Table tennis
6. Herbivores
7. Potassium
8. Whiskers
9. Gibb
10. Jellyfish
11. Denmark
12. Brazilian
13. France
14. Nancy
15. Piebald

Quiz 89

1. ROU is the international vehicle index of what country?
2. What is the real surname of actor Tom Cruise?
3. Cartoon characters Yogi Bear and Boo Boo lived where?
4. Guacamole uses which fruit?
5. What is the second highest mountain range in the world?
6. Farouk was the last king of which country?
7. Which is the largest US state?
8. Brothers Fernand, Louis and Marcel founded which motor manufacturing company?
9. Topaz is the birthstone for which month?
10. What name is given to a South American cowboy?
11. Zimbabwe was formerly called what?

12. Which battle took place south of Calais on October 25 1415?
13. Mephitis mephitis is the Latin name for which creature?
14. What is the world's most southerly capital city?
15. The movie Mrs Doubtfire starred which actor?

Quiz 89 Answers

1. Uruguay
2. Mapother
3. Jellystone Park
4. Avocado
5. Alps
6. Egypt
7. Alaska
8. Renault
9. November
10. Gaucho
11. Rhodesia
12. Agincourt
13. Skunk
14. Wellington
15. Robin Williams

Quiz 90

1. What major city is on an island in the St Lawrence River?
2. The Roman numerals XL represent which number?
3. In cartoons who provided the voice of Bugs Bunny?
4. The registration plate D is carried by cars from which country?
5. What type of puppets are those whose movements are controlled by strings?
6. The southern border of Tajikistan is formed by which country?
7. The Pentium processor for computers was developed by which company?

8. What units are used to measure sound levels?
9. British Honduras is the former name of which country?
10. Aquarius precedes which star sign?
11. Which game uses 22 balls?
12. The symbol Kr represents which gas?
13. What type of sugar is found in milk?
14. In 1962 Algeria achieved independence from which country?
15. Which William is said to have shot an apple from his son's head?

Quiz 90 Answers

1. Montreal
2. 40
3. Mel Blanc
4. Germany
5. Marionettes
6. Afghanistan
7. Intel
8. Decibels
9. Belize
10. Pisces
11. Snooker
12. Krypton
13. Lactose
14. France
15. Tell

Quiz 91

1. What is the only US state flag that still has a Union Jack on it?
2. In fiction which is Superman's home planet?
3. How many original colonies the United States were there?
4. Heaves is a disease affecting which animal?
5. Which alcoholic spirit is based on sugar cane?
6. Malaria is caused by which creature?

7. Which sign of the zodiac is represented by a bull?
8. The role of Billie Holiday in the 1972 movie Lady Sings the Blues was played by which singer?
9. A prancing horse on a yellow shield is the emblem of which car company?
10. Charles Wheatstone invented which musical instrument?
11. What was the surname of the politician who preceded John F Kennedy as the President of the USA?
12. Which is the biggest of the monkey family?
13. Who is the patron saint of travellers?
14. "The Big Yin" is the nickname of which Scottish entertainer?
15. What is the surname of the author, with the initials P.L. who wrote Mary Poppins?

Quiz 91 Answers

1. Hawaii
2. Krypton
3. 13
4. Horse
5. Rum
6. Mosquito
7. Taurus
8. Diana Ross
9. Ferrari
10. Concertina
11. Eisenhower
12. Mandrill
13. Christopher
14. Billy Connolly
15. Travers

Quiz 92

1. What was the classical standard language of ancient India?
2. Which sea is so named because it is too salty to maintain life?
3. Gertrude was the mother of which Shakespearean character?
4. Maria Kalogeropoulos is the birth name of which singer?
5. What name is given to the wild dogs found in Australia?
6. A formicary is the home of which creature?
7. The national emblem of India is which animal?
8. What is the wind instrument played by Australian Aboriginals called?
9. Where did the first Australian penal colony open?
10. Cartoon character Popeye got his power from which vegetable?
11. Belladonna is the proper name of which plant?
12. King Attila led which people?
13. What type of bean is the ingredient for baked beans?
14. Wuthering Heights was written by which of the Bronte sisters?
15. What symbol is associated with the star sign Libra?

Quiz 92 Answers

1. Sanskrit
2. Dead Sea
3. Hamlet
4. Maria Callas
5. Dingoes
6. Ant
7. Elephant
8. Didgeridoo
9. Botany Bay
10. Spinach

11. Deadly nightshade
12. Huns
13. Haricot
14. Emily
15. Scales

Quiz 93

1. What name was given to the rockets used to launch the Apollo space missions?
2. Hepatitis affects which organ?
3. Which playwright wrote Salome?
4. Who directed the movies Platoon and JFK?
5. P is the chemical symbol for which element?
6. The role of Julia Child in the 2009 movie Julia & Julia was played by which actress?
7. Which airline owned the jet that exploded over Lockerbie, Scotland in 1988?
8. The Mediterranean is connected with the Red Sea by which canal?
9. What was the real surname of actor Richard Burton?
10. Which European capital is nicknamed "the city of a hundred spires" and has tourist attractions including St Vitus Cathedral and Charles Bridge?
11. Which imperial unit of length is equal to three feet?
12. Hay Fever and Private Lives were written by which playwright?
13. Which Patricia wrote The Talented Mr Ripley?
14. A 24th wedding anniversary is represented by which precious material?
15. What is the first name of the character Rambo played by Sylvester Stallone?

Quiz 93 Answers

1. Saturn
2. Liver
3. Oscar Wilde

4. Oliver Stone
5. Phosphorus
6. Meryl Streep
7. Pan Am
8. Suez
9. Jenkins
10. Prague
11. Yard
12. Noel Coward
13. Highsmith
14. Silver
15. John

Quiz 94

1. Which animal's name is Dutch for earth pig?
2. Minnehaha was the wife of whom?
3. Which bird is noted for its boom?
4. Thriller in Manila featured what sport?
5. Plymouth Colony in America in 1620 was founded by which English settlers?
6. Which is the lightest metal?
7. What was the name of the first ship to reach Titanic after the disaster?
8. Which country was the first to give women the vote?
9. Friedrich who collaborated with Karl Marx on The Communist Manifesto had what surname?
10. The Springboks are which country's rugby union team?
11. Which country borders the Dominican Republic?
12. An island appears on which country's national flag?
13. Which 'Wonder Horse' had his own TV series?
14. Bamboo swords are used in which martial art?
15. What was the surname of the jazz composer and bandleader known as Duke?

Quiz 94 Answers

1. Aardvark
2. Hiawatha
3. Bittern
4. Boxing
5. Pilgrim Fathers
6. Lithium
7. Carpathian
8. New Zealand
9. Engels
10. South Africa
11. Haiti
12. Cyprus
13. Champion
14. Kendo
15. Ellington

Quiz 95

1. What was the given name of Stalin's daughter who defected to the US in 1967?
2. Which alcoholic drink is made from honey?
3. La Gioconda is another name for which painting?
4. The staple diet of koalas are what leaves?
5. Polynesia was owned by which literary doctor?
6. Centaurea cyanus is the Latin name of which plant?
7. Which ball game occupies the largest playing area?
8. What word is used to describe animals which can live on land or in water?
9. Who is Winnie the Pooh's donkey friend?
10. Which British city lies between the mouths of the rivers Dee and Don?
11. The source of the River Niagara is which of the Great Lakes?
12. What is the largest city in Switzerland?
13. Green tree, Indian and Burmese are varieties of which snake?

14. Which spirit is used in a Pina Colada?
15. Which element spontaneously ignites in normal air?

Quiz 95 Answers

1. Svetlana
2. Mead
3. Mona Lisa
4. Eucalyptus
5. Doolittle
6. Cornflower
7. Polo
8. Amphibian
9. Eeyore
10. Aberdeen
11. Eerie
12. Zurich
13. Python
14. Rum
15. Phosphorous

Quiz 96

1. Which actor starred in the movie version of To Kill a Mockingbird?
2. Published in 1816 which famous book is sub-titled "The Modern Prometheus"?
3. Which floor covering is made by covering canvas with linseed oil, powdered cork and rosin?
4. Vicuna is the smallest member of which animal family?
5. Which is the smallest of an orchestra's flutes?
6. What is the hardest naturally occurring substance?
7. The Swoosh logo is used by which sports company?
8. Who is the animated star of the computer game Tomb Raider?
9. Ares is the Greek God of what?
10. In 1919 who along with Brown first flew the Atlantic non-stop?

11. Which fruit derives its name from the Greek word meaning 'finger'?
12. Majorca is the largest of which islands?
13. Terra is the Roman goddess of what?
14. Which capital city means 'black pool'?
15. Which is the only one of the seven dwarfs without a beard?

Quiz 96 Answers

1. Gregory Peck
2. Frankenstein
3. Linoleum
4. Camel
5. Piccolo
6. Diamond
7. Nike
8. Lara Croft
9. War
10. Alcock
11. Date
12. Balearic
13. The Earth
14. Dublin
15. Dopey

Quiz 97

1. Muhammad was born in which city?
2. The name of which car manufacturer means People's Car?
3. Which Canadian province is named after one of Queen Victoria's daughters?
4. Who led the Sioux against General Custer at the Battle of Little Big Horn?
5. The Japanese alcoholic drink Sake is made from what?
6. Which land measurement was originally the size that a yoke of oxen could pull in a day?

7. Which Gary played the role of Sid Vicious in the 1986 movie Sid and Nancy?
8. Aneroid and mercury are versions of which measuring device?
9. Which precious gem is green in colour?
10. Pb is the chemical symbol of which metal?
11. Which is the nearest planet to the sun?
12. Only continent is occupied by a single nation, which is it?
13. Which independent island is Australia's nearest neighbour to the west?
14. Sullivan who wrote operettas with Gilbert had what first name?
15. Which is the world's second smallest state?

Quiz 97 Answers

1. Mecca
2. Volkswagen
3. Alberta
4. Sitting Bull
5. Rice
6. Acre
7. Oldman
8. Barometer
9. Emerald
10. Lead
11. Mercury
12. Australia
13. Mauritius
14. Arthur
15. Monaco

Quiz 98

1. Which is the largest county in the Republic of Ireland?
2. "You must remember this, a kiss is just a kiss" is a line from which song?
3. Which ghost ship is the theme of an 1841 Richard Wagner opera?
4. After all, tomorrow is another day" is the last line of which movie?
5. "Anna Karenina" and "War and Peace" were written by which Russian author?
6. Quinine is best known for preventing which disease?
7. Which flower is also called a flag?
8. Ava Gardner was one of the wives of which eight times married actor?
9. Which country has the world's longest coastline?
10. The movie 'Gladiator' was directed by whom?
11. Which is the only sign of the zodiac to start and finish with the same letter?
12. Literary detective Sam Spade was created by which author?
13. Which mountain range extends through Morocco, Algeria and Tunisia?
14. Diced apples, celery and walnuts in mayonnaise are ingredients of which salad?
15. Which is the best-known university in Paris?

Quiz 98 Answers

1. Cork
2. "As Time Goes By"
3. Flying Dutchman
4. Gone With the Wind
5. Leo Tolstoy
6. Malaria
7. Iris
8. Mickey Rooney
9. Canada

10. Ridley Scott
11. Sagittarius
12. Dashell Hammett
13. Atlas
14. Waldorf
15. Sorbonne

Quiz 99

1. Which South American animal is a relation of the camel?
2. A paddle steamer called the Cotton Blossom features in which musical?
3. Which insect gives its name to a swimming stroke?
4. What was the surname of the Professor who was Sherlock Holmes's greatest enemy?
5. Discovered by Abel Tasman in 1643 which group of islands was ceded to Britain in 1874?
6. Which mythical beast had a lion's body and an eagle's head, wings and claws?
7. What name is given to a long, loose hooded robe with full sleeves worn by men in Muslim countries?
8. Which edifice stands on the banks of the River Jumna at Agra?
9. Trappist monks maintain an order of what?
10. The Centennial State is the nickname for which US state?
11. In which year was Neptune first located?
12. What was the name of the ship Ernest Shackleton abandoned during his 1914-16 Antarctic expedition?
13. Which is the largest of the Trucial states?
14. Digitalis is the Latin name for which wild flower?
15. Which Russian word means 'Openness'?

Quiz 99 Answers

1. Llama
2. Showboat
3. Butterfly
4. Moriarty
5. Fiji
6. Griffin
7. Djellaba
8. Taj Mahal
9. Silence
10. Colorado
11. 1846
12. Endurance
13. Abu Dhabi
14. Foxglove
15. Glasnost

Quiz 100

1. Which word can be a musical instrument and a tall narrow glass?
2. In which US city is the John F. Kennedy airport?
3. From which language does the word anorak come?
4. Which North African seaport's name is Spanish for white house?
5. To which famous person was Anne Hathaway married?
6. Which country's name means 'City of Lions'?
7. Who is the British equivalent of the USA's Uncle Sam?
8. In 1954, which athlete first broke the 4-minute mile?
9. True or false the Iron Age preceded the Bronze Age?
10. Which US state lies between Canada and Wyoming?
11. In music terminology what does the word presto mean?
12. A water moccasin is what type of creature?
13. Which vegetable is used in sauerkraut?
14. In chess by what other name is the castle known?
15. Which South American country has borders with Columbia and Peru?

Quiz 100 Answers

1. Flute
2. New York
3. Eskimo
4. Casablanca
5. William Shakespeare
6. Singapore
7. John Bull
8. Roger Bannister
9. False – the Iron Age followed the Bronze
10. Montana
11. Quickly
12. Snake
13. Cabbage
14. Rook
15. Ecuador